Ruth Lynford My Life in Design

Ruth Lynford My Life in Design

Written by Marlene Ann Birkman

Designed by Kiku Obata & Company

Published by Autobiographical Publishing
Company Pty Ltd.

Dedicated to
Ruth's children—
Jeffrey, Lance, Leslye, and Lloyd—
and all of her grandchildren

Published in Australia in 2013 by
Autobiographical Publishing Company Pty Ltd
ABN 89 059 734 431

Copyright © Autobiographical Publishing Company Pty Ltd 2013
Autobiographical Publishing Company Pty Ltd Reference Number: 1084

All rights reserved. Apart from any fair dealing for the purposes of private study,
research, criticism, or review, as permitted under the Copyright Act, no part of this
publication may be reproduced, stored in a retrieval system, or transmitted in any
form by any means, electronic, mechanical, photocopying, recording, or otherwise,
without the written permission of the publisher or author.

National Library of Australia Cataloguing-in-Publication entry:

Author:	Birkman, Marlene Ann
Title:	Ruth Lynford : my life in design / Marlene Ann Birkman
ISBN:	9781864705164 (hbk)
Subjects:	Interior decorators—United States—Biography
	Interior decoration—United States—History—20th century
	Interior decoration—United States—History—21st century
	Architecture, domestic—United States—20th century
	Architecture, domestic—United States—21st century
Dewey Number:	729.092273

Designed by Kiku Obata & Company
Published by Autobiographical Publishing Company Pty Ltd
Printed by Everbest Printing Co. Ltd in Hong Kong/China on 150gsm Lumi Silk

Table of Contents

8	Foreword
10	Preface
17	Chapter One: Form
37	Chapter Two: Unity and Variety
61	Chapter Three: Light
79	Chapter Four: Color
91	Chapter Five: Emphasis
101	Chapter Six: Rhythm
109	Chapter Seven: Harmony
117	Chapter Eight: Balance
131	Chapter Nine: Texture and Shape
142	Representative List of Projects
145	Awards and Recognition
147	Acknowledgements
149	Photography Credits

Foreword

Ask an architect or design professional, and s/he will tell others that to be an expert designer is to be multitalented. This requires embodying a myriad of skills and wearing many hats. It is also well known that being a good designer requires an innate curiosity and ability to problem solve, a depth of multitudinous literacies and, often, many years of experience. Most of all, those acclaimed as gifted design professionals demonstrate leadership that is grounded in the conceptual and the beautiful and which, simultaneously, informs the present and the future. These individuals play a critical role in helping us build and navigate to a better place in society and culture. By identifying fresh possibilities of exploration and taking a lead along new and unformed pathways, these individuals help to provide direction for investigation and advancement. They are substantial, well-rounded people and they, and their work, have a profound impact on our lives and the environments we occupy. In our time, Ruth Lynford is such a designer.

Design, today, touted as the creative industry of the 21st century, has become serious business and a household word. For Ruth, with her sixty-five-plus years of work in design, this is nothing new. Design and the profession have always been serious and important, and a way of life beyond lifestyle considerations. Inherently, Ruth is a pioneer, which may not be entirely surprising given that she hails from St. Louis on the Mississippi, which was once considered the Gateway to the West. After studying architecture there, she shifted her focus to the design of interiors. In this, she expanded her work beyond the practice by also taking charge of advocacy for the profession in New York State. Believing interior design to be a legitimate discipline with professional responsibilities, she envisioned making it a fully recognized and state licensed profession. Reflecting her own career and experience as a practicing designer in the postwar decades, she has persistently strived to establish the bona fides of the discipline and to have its legitimacy formally recognized. She believes – with good reason – that the interior designer, as an expert, needs to be seen as a full partner in the process of making beautiful and supportive designs of the built environment. In this, Ruth has tenaciously worked to help clarify, educate, legitimize, and advocate for a wholesome discipline.

Often the term "leading designer" gets used to reflect the designer's view of an expression of the avant-garde. This can be an expression of good taste and the fashionable. However, to appreciate leadership at an intellectual and social level requires the designer to be at the "cutting edge" of the discipline and to care passionately about the impact and consequence of his/her actions. Leading for social change is often non-glamorous and beset with repeated disappointment. It is also most often thankless. It requires having vision, nerves of steel, and the strongest sense of self and purpose. Above all, it requires a die-hard belief in the possibility of the greater public good. This is what Ruth Lynford exemplifies and continues to espouse. She has been staunchly resolute in her convictions and has worked tirelessly to further expansion, growth, and respect, both for her profession, as well as for society's understanding and appreciation of them. She has helped to shape these perceptions by leading simultaneously from the frontline and from behind.

In her lifetime, Ruth has lived fully and bridged the acceptance of the female professional in the contemporary workplace. Historically, women have played an intrinsic and critical role in the evolution of design. Generations of women design leaders, including such iconic figures as Edith Wharton and Florence Knoll, are prime examples of having helped to push forward and establish new and significant frontiers. In our generation, Ruth Lynford, an industry icon, is one of these great and exceptional industry figureheads. The most remarkable thing about Ruth Lynford is not the contributions she has made to those near and dear to her and to her life's work as a designer, but that she lives and breathes what she designs. She is a quintessential designer in the broadest sense of the term. She walks the talk of the principles of design, to the extent that it is possible, as she so elegantly embodies design. For her, design is not a mere theory or a simple credo; it is a goal to be accomplished. All who know Ruth know that she has met that goal better than anyone else in the profession today.

Before you in this fascinating book is the proof of that achievement. It tells the life story of a deeply caring and cosmopolitan woman, someone who on the one hand is real and down-to-earth, and on the other is a true visionary and an idealist. She may be petite in physical stature, but she takes giant steps forward to transform the ordinary into the extraordinary as she leads with her poise and elegance.

Shashi Caan
Founding Principal, The Collective US/UK
President, The International Federation of Interior Architects/Designers (IFI),
2009–2011, 2011–2013

Preface

As children, we were always eager to create a tent, fort, or most of all, a leaf house. With rakes in hand and imaginations soaring, we Indiana neighborhood kids went to work. After a long day of shaping a perimeter with elm leaves, we crossed our threshold and carried in and arranged dishes, tables, blankets, toys, books, and bicycles. In that dream house, the play began and we transformed our worlds. Never, did I envision that years later, Ruth Lynford would show me the why and wonder of design.

Heading to lunch after a good night's sleep at the Savoy Hotel, Mary Strauss, two friends, and I were about to meet Ruth Lynford. It was our first, full day taking in the marvels of London. For me, Ruth was about to become one of them.

Mary had invited several St. Louis "girls" on an overseas adventure for her birthday. As a Fox Partner, she included in our itinerary the opening night of Fox Theatricals' production of *Thoroughly Modern Millie* at the Shaftesbury Theatre. We were elated. Terry Lynford was particularly excited because we were about to dine with her Aunt Ruthie, who had stopped off in London after a trip to Paris with her daughter, Leslye. Over the years, Terry had related tales about her New York Aunt Ruthie and cousins, Jeff, Lance, Leslye, and Lloyd. She did so with such warmth and animation, that even though I had never met them, I secretly wanted each of them to be part of my family. Over time, I, too, soon found myself also referring to Ruth as "Aunt Ruthie."

The four of us walked into the San Lorenzo Restaurant. Amidst the quiet elegance and potted palms, there she was—Terry's aunt, unlike any other aunt that I had ever known or read about. Aunt Ruthie appeared to be the embodiment of Hollywood glamour, the kind I spotted in *Photoplay* or *Modern Screen* during my youth in the 1950s. Petite and sleek, with big, brown eyes and long, dark hair, she exuded poise and polish. She was beauty and style all in one. Unknowingly, on that autumn Monday in 2003, I stepped into another kind of opening.

During the following few years when I occasionally accompanied Mary Strauss on theater trips, we met up with Aunt Ruthie for lunch in Manhattan. Although I knew she was an architect and interior designer, born and raised in St. Louis, our conversations rarely touched on that. Instead, we happily chatted about New York, museums, travel, and relationships.

In St. Louis, our friendship continued when Aunt Ruthie came for meetings and visits with her grandsons at Washington University. She then often invited her cousin Clarice, niece Terry, Mary, and me for brunch. After each reunion, I admired Aunt Ruthie's zest and being, not to mention her love for desserts, which seemed not to affect her eighty-nine pounds.

On November 6, 2010, Ruth received a Distinguished Alumni Award at the Washington University Founders Day celebration at the St. Louis Union Station Marriott Hotel. Along with family members, Mary Strauss and I were also invited. That evening, David McCullough, historian and Pulitzer Prize winner, spoke compellingly about the American character and the well-lived life.

Afterwards, sitting at a large, round table, between Terry and Tondra Lynford, I listened to the reading of Ruth's commendation, detailing her achievements in interior design and education. For me, most striking was that she founded her own design firm after being told by a principal at York & Sawyer that women were not allowed out in the field or in the design studio. She then continued her stride forward, by founding the Interior Designers for Legislation in New York (IDLNY) and New York Eleven. At that moment, I realized that Ruth Lynford was and is, indeed, an American character, cut from fine cloth, not linsey-woolsey. Her life is one of both daring and design.

With an interest in folklore and narrative, I sat riveted, ready to know more about her. Inspired by McCullough's words, I was eager to ask: "Who are you? Who are your people?" At the end of the ceremony, I congratulated Ruth and inquired, "Have you ever written your story?" She shook her head and smiled. I exclaimed, "You are a trailblazer with a tale to be told." During that evening, I saw her anew. She was both person and professional; I could no longer call her "Aunt Ruthie."

In January, Ruth called me and said, "I have been thinking about what you said and wonder if you might help me write about my life?" I accepted, knowing, of course, that to keep up with her, my pace would have to quicken. I wanted Ruth to narrate her own story. Set to go, she explained, "My mind is like a kaleidoscope. There's no stop."

During the spring of 2011, guided by questions and with tape recorders in hand, I began the interviewing process in St. Louis at Washington University, the Ritz-Carlton Hotel, and the Chase Park Plaza. I then flew to Manhattan several times to continue the dialogue. It was in New York, as I walked in her steps, that the pieces of her life came together.

With her, I went out on the town to meet Tom Della Corte, her hair designer, and to dinner at the Metropolitan Club and Rouge Tomate. We enjoyed *Anything Goes* and *The Sensational Josephine Baker* and experienced a magnificent dinner party at the home of her friends, the Kunstadts. We heard a lecture by David Garred Lowe on Americans in Paris, sponsored by the Beaux Arts Alliance in conjunction with the French Heritage Society. We also had dinner with friends and attended Washington University's annual alumni banquet at the Harmonie Club.

It was in her Fifth Avenue apartment, however, that Ruth became most vivid. Her haven of light space reflects the calm that she radiates. Classical music fills the air. The entrance hall and living room are accented by two-thousand-year-old, Roman and Etruscan artifacts. An 1860s Japanese silk kimono, from the end of the Edo Period graces one wall. Carefully placed pieces of contemporary art, including an abstract lithograph by Joan Mitchell, delight the eye. In this tranquil space, line meets form; the effect is both subtle and striking.

In her bedroom, a Japanese screen dating from the 1630s depicts the story of a statesman as a little boy at the beginning of the Edo Period. Family pictures and orchid plants line the window built-ins overlooking Central Park. Walls of beige, as well as earth-colored fabrics and furniture, convey peace. From room to room, the past flows smoothly into the present.

In her home office, Ruth perches on a black leather and chrome swivel desk chair next to the window. Though sitting, she is on the move. With her phone, laptop, and line-up of seven clear plastic trays labeled—IDLNY, New York Eleven Plus, ICIS, Washington University, Theater, Restaurant, and Current—before her, she meets the day. While I am preparing for the interview, rummaging through papers I stacked on the rust-colored, leather seat of a nearby chair, I suddenly remember that it is eighteenth-century French Regency, and museum quality, and I relocate the papers neatly on the floor.

Finished answering e-mails and phone messages, Ruth, dressed in a black-and-white kaftan from Leslye, moves over to a small sofa. Sitting under a sixteenth-century Indian temple hanging, we, with eyes on the future, begin the taping. We become immersed.

Two hours later, it is time to take a break and for Ruth to get dressed. She changes into a pair of white satin palazzo pants, a floral silk top with a matching belt, slips into gold slippers with tapestry heels, puts on a double strand of pearls, and is ready for lunch. After a few minutes in the kitchen, with her usual grace and aplomb, she carries two plates with salmon salad placed in avocado halves to the table, already set for two. "May I bring you another drink?" she asks. "No, thank you. I have everything," I answer, as I look around, and realize that, in fact, I really do. On my plate, next to the salad are a few slices of bread-and-butter pickles, a traditional Midwestern garnish, a staple. Ruth remarks, "I love these pickles. No one in New York seems to know about them." Her words affirm what I discovered in our cheerful exploration. At her core, Ruth is truly bread-and-butter pickles. Without pretense, her passion for life and design is part of her unwavering desire to bring the best to each of us. As a child, she liked to iron clothes; as an adult, she works to rid the wrinkles from the day. Through and through, Ruth is at one with design. With her, I feel at home.

Over many months, I observed her look to the future as she visited with and assisted young student-architects and designers, offering ideas, information, support, and readings. From her, I learned that a healthy, safe, and sustainable environment fosters personal and universal growth and well-being. I experienced, once again, that pleasing places lift the spirit and offer pleasure to the people who inhabit them.

Humble and unassuming, Ruth Lynford is bread-and-butter, style and substance. As one small person, she has made one large footprint. Hers is the mark of an American spirit, outside and in the world of design.

Marlene Ann Birkman

"EVEN BEFORE
I BECAME
INVOLVED IN
DESIGN, I WAS
INVOLVED."

Chapter One: Form

My beginnings unfold in the heartland, St. Louis, Missouri—"The Gateway to the West." Not surprisingly, they involve matters of the heart, the romance between Adolph Kahn and Dorothy Sacks, my parents. Their union was not without intrigue.

Simon and Tiertza Sacks, my maternal grandparents, had five children: one boy, Isadore, and four girls: Jenny, Annie, Dorothy, and Sarah. I do not know if it was an Orthodox Jewish custom or one of the 1920s, but the women in a family had to wed in the order of their ages. As I was told, my mother, Dorothy, the third daughter, was the first one to find a beau, Adolph, whom she met at a Thanksgiving eve dance. Because of her birth order, she could not reveal her engagement until her sisters Jenny and Annie married.

On Jenny's wedding day to Michael Blumenfeld, Simon and Tiertza announced my parents' betrothal. Mysteriously, a sudden switch of ages occurred. My mother became the second-oldest daughter and Annie, unmarried, the third. My Grandfather Sacks, a sweet and gentle man, worked as a tailor. Either he was exceptionally skilled at fitting pieces together, or that was how things were done in those days.

Before my mother, Dorothy Sacks, and father, Adolph Kahn, united, they needed to locate housing. My paternal grandmother, Rosa Kahn, whose husband Newman had been deceased for many years, owned a good deal of St. Louis real estate and even built two houses on California Avenue. Born in St. Louis, she was a spirited businesswoman, who did not believe in banks, and carried her money in a little gray cloth, pull-string purse. Each morning, she put the string over her head and around her neck and kept the bag carefully tucked inside her blouse.

My father told my mother that he had heard of a place for them to live, a two-family flat at 3710 Bamberger Avenue, and asked her to take a look at it. Because of the difficulty of finding an apartment in 1922, my mother went to see it. At the time, tenants, the Rudloffs, lived upstairs. She spoke to Mrs. Rudloff and asked, "This is lovely. Who owns it?" Mrs. Rudloff replied, "Mrs. Kahn," my mother's future mother-in-law. So when my mother and father married on February 26, 1922, they moved downstairs and paid rent. Shortly before, my father's brother, Roland Kahn, who was already married, moved upstairs. Two years later on July 3, 1924, my uncle Rollie and aunt Dora were blessed with twin girls, Norma and Hortense Kahn.

Soon after, I was born on September 17, 1924, at St. Joseph's Hospital and named Ruth Bettye Kahn. The name Blanche had been chosen for me in honor of my father's favorite sister who died at the age of eight, but somehow "Ruth" prevailed. Jubilant about his six-pound offspring, my father boasted that "Kahn" meant "little boat" in German. On that day, my joy-filled journey began.

My father gave me the gift of a strong self-image and a zest for living. He was never bored a day in his life. I became very close to him. A college graduate and certified public accountant, he was the only one of the Kahn family to complete college, by attending Saint Louis University at night. Only three of his eleven siblings grew to maturity. His older brother Herbie married Emma and they had no children. My father was next, then came my aunt Alma and uncle Rollie.

My father rented an office downtown in the Wainwright Building and worked diligently preparing taxes, which in those days needed to be filed by March fifteenth. While he was busy with numbers, my mother, often called an "income tax widow," and I headed off to the movies at the Melba Theater on Grand Avenue. My mother loved the cinema. One night when we arrived home from a film, we discovered that our house had been burglarized. Among the items taken was a box containing three tiny silver rings, each with a different stone—a diamond, sapphire, and ruby—given to me at my birth by a client of my father's, who was a jeweler. Inside the box was a letter that read, "Dear Blanche, You do not know me now, but someday I hope you will." This note was a tribute not only to me, but also to my father.

At age three-and-a-half, I was a short, petite child with a rather low voice, so my father sent me to study

Ruth, age eight months. Ruth was born on September 17, 1924, at St. Joseph's Hospital and named Ruth Bettye Kahn. The name Blanche had been chosen for her in honor of her father's favorite sister, but somehow "Ruth" prevailed.

Previous page: Dorothy and Adolph Kahn

elocution. I took to it like a duck does to water. Soon after, when my sister Gloria was born, my Grandmother Kahn took me to the lessons. She sat at the end of the long room where I recited, and in full voice shouted, "Louder, Ruthie, louder." For performances, I dressed up in many costumes including my Sis Hopkins and ballet outfits.

During childhood, Norma, Hortense, Gloria, and I enjoyed frolicking in our backyard, which to us seemed enormous. We also had fun playing in a small space in an extension under our porch that had a little cubicle with a window leading down to the basement. One day, Gloria impulsively banged the glass with a wooden stick; it shattered and cut her in the neck. My parents rushed her to the hospital at the corner of Grand and Chippewa. Luckily, the wound was not serious. After the injury, my mother, father, aunt, and uncle blamed me and the twins for the incident. They never replaced the glass.

In time, my uncle Rollie, aunt Dora, and the girls moved to University City, and the Rudloffs, the previous renters, moved back upstairs. Although they had no children, Mr. Rudloff's younger sister, Edna, lived with them. Mr. Rudloff or "Hubby," as my parents affectionately called him, tended our entire lawn and flower garden.

The seven of us lived together in the two-family brick flat. Every week Mrs. Rudloff, my mother, and I took turns scrubbing our four stone front steps with a stiff bristle wooden brush. We then dried each step with a clean cloth. My mother said, "Ruthie, we have to keep everything tidy."

At our home, we had only one bedroom, so Gloria and I had daily duties. Each evening, we carefully wheeled our rollaway beds out of the dining room closet; each morning, we folded and tucked them neatly back into storage. With an eye for design, I also took charge of arranging our furniture, moving lamps, tables, and chairs at whim from place to place. Fortunately, my mother was easy going and cheerfully accepted my burgeoning proclivity.

During first grade, my interests widened. When one of my friends who owned a dog with puppies asked, "Would you like to have one?" I answered, "Oh, I would love a puppy." In my two hands, I then gingerly carried it home. My mother took one look at its white fluffy coat and warned, "You're going to have to wait until your father comes home to see if you can keep it." When my father arrived, he said, "No, you can't keep her. Hubby takes such good care of our garden that it just wouldn't be fair to him." So Gloria and I, with tears rolling down our faces, gave up our bounty. Amazingly, in later years, my parents bought a Boston Bull Terrier named Pal.

When I was eight, our family celebrated my Grandmother Kahn's seventieth birthday by hosting a glamorous party at night. Japanese lanterns shimmered in

Ruth Kahn in 1932, age nine. For programs, Ruth dressed in many costumes including her Sis Hopkins and ballet outfits.

our rose garden. Everything glowed and everyone was joyous. My grandmother beamed. I had heard that all grandmothers say, "You are my favorite," but I knew that I definitely was, because whenever Grandmother Kahn came to our house to visit, she always gave me coins.

My two grandmothers provided an interesting contrast. On Sunday evenings, I, as a little girl, went with my family to my maternal Grandmother Sacks's apartment on Eastgate off Delmar. For supper, we purchased corned beef and coleslaw from a delicatessen across the alleyway and for dessert, we bought glazed donuts from Pratzel's Bakery. My mother's family, the Sacks, emigrated from Lithuania and then moved to London, England. When my mother was six months old, they settled in St. Louis, where her parents had relatives. My Grandmother Sacks came from an Orthodox Jewish family and kept a kosher home.

My father's family, the Kahns, originally from Germany, moved to St. Louis in the early 1800s. In 1852, they, with others, founded B'nai El Temple, the first Jewish Reform Congregation west of the Mississippi, where I was raised, consecrated at four, and confirmed. So I had one grandmother who belonged to an Orthodox congregation and kept kosher, and another who was a Reformed Jew, who attended a reform congregation and cooked ham. At Passover, my Grandmother Sacks held the Seder. Short and plump, she always wore her apron over a housedress. My Grandmother Kahn appeared in an elegant, gray silk dress adorned with a long string of pearls around her neckline. For Gloria and me, having these two grandmothers at the same table proved to be formative.

Living in a predominately Gentile neighborhood in South St. Louis also shaped us. When Gloria was about six years old, she often went upstairs to the Rudloffs. One day she noticed some rosary beads that were on the table

20 | My Life in Design

and asked, "What are these beads for?" Mrs. Rudloff answered, "We use them to say our prayers." A few days later, Gloria climbed the steps again to see the beads. She picked them up, carefully placed them in her hands, and little by little quietly spoke, "Shema Yisrael, Adonai Eloheinu, Adonai Echad," a Hebrew prayer she knew in English. Mrs. Rudloff, of course, repeated this to my mother. Similarly curious, I often attended the neighborhood Catholic church with Edna, Mr. Rudloff's younger sister. Although I enjoyed both being with Edna and the majesty of the sanctuary, I did not understand a word of the service, spoken mostly in Latin. So, day-by-day, we sisters at a young age, discovered other cultures.

In my early years, I became increasingly clothes-conscious. Realizing this, my mother allowed me to go downtown by myself on the streetcar to Famous-Barr Department Store to buy a snowsuit. I spotted a brown wool one, with a white knitted neck with an orange and brown band. It had a zipper running on the diagonal, instead of straight up and down. Using my mother's charge card, I made the purchase and proudly rode home on the streetcar with the suit. On a later shopping adventure, I went downtown to Klein's Department Store, saw a red velvet dress with a white lace collar and red buttons, bought it, and took it home to show Mrs. Rudloff, a very fine seamstress. She copied it and I returned the dress.

I observed that other children wore what their parents selected for them and were content. I, however, was particular about what my mother put on me. When she dressed my sister and me alike, I wanted the frock trimmed in blue, Gloria could have the same one, trimmed in red. Occasionally, I wore hand-me-downs from my aunt Jenny's daughter, Clarice Blumenfeld. I remember one, in particular, that I cherished, a blue and white organdy dress with a matching belt that I wore at my aunt Annie's wedding. I noticed design in everything. I looked at design everywhere. It was part of me.

Throughout childhood, my fondness for elocution lessons continued, so my parents decided to transfer me to Forbes Studio on Delmar Avenue at the end of the streetcar line. In preparation for my lessons, my mother often read the words aloud to me. In 1933, when Mrs. Forbes was asked to suggest children to perform in *Rip Van Winkle,* at The Muny Opera in Forest Park, she said that her son and I were "talented at talking." The two of us were then given speaking roles in the production. I was elated. Unexpectedly, at the age of nine, I received my first paycheck—seven dollars for seven days of work. My mother cashed it. To this day, I wish she had framed it instead.

Top: Rosa and Neuman Kahn, mother and father of Adolph Kahn.
Bottom: Dorothy Sacks

With savings of about eighteen dollars, I was encouraged by my parents to study piano. We purchased a player piano with pedals that when pumped turned rolls, and I began lessons at a school on Grand Avenue. Sometime later, a very stern, staccato-like woman came to our home to teach me. Although I did not like her much or practice often, I actually accomplished quite a lot. Sitting on the piano bench, I played Gabriel Morel's *The Norwegian Cradle Song,* my favorite piece, over and over. My mother, who had an innate sense of music, also played the piano, but by ear. Unlike me, she possessed a strong singing voice and frequently sang an aria from Giacomo Puccini's *Madama Butterfly.* Ever busy with performances and piano scales, I was also eager to be with my friends.

Eva Ruth Grimm was my best girlfriend in the neighborhood. Each morning, she came over to get me to walk with her to Rose Fanning Public School. Inevitably, I was late. I liked to sleep. My father would say, "Ruth, you'll sleep your life away." At grammar school, I developed such a vivid imagination that during the Christmas season, the teachers asked me to create a play. Where the ideas came from, I do not know. Always dutifully prepared with my homework, I was aware that the teachers catered to me.

In the early grades, my father helped me with my school assignments, but it finally reached the point at which I said, "Dad, I can do these by myself." I wrote my own essays, I achieved, and I loved school. At report card time, my parents had a unique arrangement: my father signed my report card as long as I had all A's. If I had one B, my mother signed it. Fortunately, for me, my father did most of the signing.

After graduating from the eighth grade, I attended Roosevelt High School in South St. Louis, where I was one of only five Jewish students in a school of two thousand.

Even though I shined academically and dressed beautifully, I was never invited to join any clubs. One day, my homeroom teacher took me aside and quietly told me that she felt that the reason for my not being accepted into the extra-curricular activities was because of anti-Semitism. Nonetheless, I moved forward with grace and resolve.

Still fascinated with elocution at fifteen, I began teaching it at home, offering either class or private lessons to children from ages four to eight. To advertise, Gloria placed slips of paper under people's doors in our neighborhood. The money that I earned from teaching, I put away for college.

During free time, wearing a long, taffeta, aqua gown, I continued doing performances for the public. At one of the programs, I noticed a handsome young man, much older than I, singing *Too Tired to Say Good Night*. He attracted me more than I had ever imagined possible.

I also became active in theater groups, especially the YMHA—Young Men's Hebrew Association—on Union Avenue. There I met Nathan Garson, six years my senior, who looked like Errol Flynn. I fell madly in love with him. One Sunday morning without calling in advance, he drove to Bamberger Avenue to see me. As I sat playing the piano in my pajamas, my mother announced, "Nathan is outside." I shouted, "Mother, I have to get dressed." While he waited, she entertained him.

A year or so later, Nathan was drafted into the service and stationed in Little Rock, Arkansas. Before he left, we were at the Y and he said softly, "I want to kiss you goodbye." I had never been kissed by a boy before and did not know what to do. He then held me in his arms, kissed me on the lips, and off he went. During the summer, when his older sister, Hannah, and older brother, Howard, planned to visit him in a Little Rock Army barrack, they invited me to join them. I selected my travel attire, a one-piece, piquet, white-skirted dress with a pastel-colored top. In Little Rock, Nathan and I smooched a lot, then I went home. Soon after, he was sent to Alaska, where he remained for many years. In the interim, we corresponded.

Shortly before I turned sixteen, my parents decided to move. During the house-hunting, I took a leading role in advising my father. "That's the one we should buy." I suggested upon seeing a lovely, spacious place in University City. My father, however, did not make decisions quickly; he was analytical. By the time he decided to look at the house again, it had, of course, been sold. I then found another home at 7811 Cornell in University City, a two-story, brick house with oak floors. The first floor had a living room, dining room, kitchen, back porch, and powder room. The second floor had three bedrooms: two good-sized rooms, and a smaller one used as a den, and a large bathroom. The four of us moved in.

Form | 23

Knowingly, I chose the floor coverings and placed the furniture. I selected a beige carpet for the stairway and the three bedrooms, and located area rugs for the dining and living rooms. I then convinced my mother to purchase a new sofa, because our large brown mohair one was outdated. At Lammert's Department Store, I discovered a Duncan Phyfe sofa with a striking rose damask upholstery and a side chair. For the bedroom I shared with my sister, I decided on modern furniture, twin beds in light wood and a large mirror at the dressing table. As a teenager, my instinct for interiors took hold.

My father believed that women should be college educated the same as men, and that they should be educated not only in liberal arts, but also in a profession. He said, "Ruth, you must have two years of liberal arts and then a profession, any profession that you want." He continued, "I hope you get married, have lots of children, but you never know in this life when you might lose all your toys—all your possessions." Pointing to his head, he explained, "You must be prepared. What's in your head, you never lose." I heard him; I had to focus on a career. I thought that I wanted to be an actress and had won a four-year scholarship to Northwestern University. Ultimately, as the older daughter and only sixteen, I had two choices: my father's alma mater, Saint Louis University in midtown, at that time with no campus, or Washington University. I chose Washington University with its beautiful campus.

In early September, 1940, I entered Washington University and lived at home. My father, who taught me to drive when I was fifteen, took the bus to go downtown to his office, allowing me to use our Chevrolet to drive to school. At the end of the first year, my mother, who from time to time suffered from bouts of depression, became severely despondent and experienced what was then called a "nervous breakdown." In the morning after Gloria

Opposite page: Ruth Kahn
dressed for a performance

left for University City High School, my mother would cry out, "Please, don't leave me." I felt compelled to stay with her. Not knowing how to deal with her condition, my father said, "Lack of discipline, you know." Finally, she had to be hospitalized and given shock treatments. For several months, her wavering health affected my study habits, class attendance, and day-to-day well-being.

Although my mother was bright and had a very pleasant nature, I do not know if she ever completed high school. I do know that she felt honored to have married a native-born, World War I veteran, and college graduate from a prominent Jewish family. At times, however, she seemed embarrassed about her mother's limited English skills and Yiddish accent. In contrast, my father had great respect for his family, especially his younger sister, Alma, who at sixteen made her debut with a "coming-out party." Alma was a terrific cook. My father often asked my mother, "Why can't you do things like Alma?" Although my mother's cooking was fine, she lacked confidence in herself and sometimes, I think, felt inferior.

After completing two years of liberal arts "on the hill" at Washington University, I needed to decide on a profession. I excelled in mathematics, but was unclear about a career direction. When May Kahn, my father's cousin by marriage, heard about my math agility, she said, "Ruth, you should go into architecture." Washington University, of course, had a very fine School of Architecture "down the hill" at Givens Hall.

With nothing else to pursue, I enrolled. I was pleased to discover that Professor Paul Valenti, who specialized in design, offered a course on interiors and delighted that architect Gene Mackey would be my mentor and advisor. Professor Mackey explained to me that after a student completed the first year, a committee examined each student's ability to design. The evaluation was not based on grades,

Ruth Kahn, far right, in dance line. Even at a young age, Ruth was into fashion, as seen by her white shoes.

but on the potential to continue and complete the five-year program. I thought, "Oh, heavens, I don't know if I will make it." Concerned that I did not have the requisite talent, I approached Professor Mackey who told me, "Ruth, stop worrying. If ever there was anyone who had the ability, you do." Soon after, I passed the scrutiny of the committee and was accepted. The freshman class had approximately seventy students; only five were women.

In the design studio, each student had a space with a large drawing board, a T-square, and a triangle. My seat was by a window on the second floor of Givens Hall, facing Forsyth Avenue. Professor Lawrence Hill, the Dean, who specialized in the Beaux Arts, taught classes on history and perspective. Young architects from Massachusetts Institute of Technology led by Professor Joe Murphy taught the Bauhaus. The fact that I was not schizophrenic being taught Beaux Arts and Bauhaus concurrently is a miracle. As a result, I am able to design traditional, as well as modern interiors, and am equally comfortable with both. I credit Washington University for providing that professional equilibrium.

During the program, we had *charrettes*, which often lasted until two o'clock in the morning. To fortify myself, I brought grapefruits from home and bought Baby Ruth bars from the candy machine in Givens Hall. It was an exhilarating time, complemented by Gyo Obata and a small group of Japanese American students, who were permitted to study at Washington University while their parents and families were interned in camps. Gyo's father, Chiura Obata, a renowned California artist, occasionally mailed small watercolors done on silk from Topaz, Utah, which Gyo brought to class for all of us to see. At that time, I had no idea of his father's acclaim.

Outside of school, I met Irving Kopakin, years older, although I did not know it. We began dating. A sergeant from Chicago, stationed at Jefferson Barracks, Irv was free to come and go anytime he wanted. He fell in love with me. I was nineteen. I told him, "I'm madly in love with Nathan Garson and he's in Alaska." He said, "That's all right. We'll go out anyway." For our dates, I bought black and white fabrics and had identical garments made by a University City dressmaker. Irv "wined and dined" me. He even treated me to evenings at The Muny, in Forest Park, where we sat outdoors in box seats and later had dinner. Afterwards, my mother cautioned, "Ruth, he's older than you think." I added, "He likes to sing *Embraceable You*," which impressed my mother who knew all of the Gershwin songs from an earlier era. Then I saw his birth date on his driver's license and, sure enough, Irv was eleven years older. Concerned that he and I might wed, my mother commented, "Just because I married a short man, you don't have to!" I said, "Oh, mother, you are right."

During college, I became a student member of the American Society of Interior Designers. The annual convention was being held in Chicago, so my mother and I planned a trip there. Irv said, "Oh, you must visit my parents," whom I had already met. In time, I realized that I was not in love with him.

Not long after the Chicago visit, I received a letter from Nathan who had been transferred to Fort Benning Officer Training. He wrote, "Come down, and we'll get married." I was excited, but afraid to tell my parents, so I showed the letter to Rabbi Julian Miller, my confidant. He counseled, "The war is almost over. You can wait until then." I was almost ready to graduate from Washington University. Nathan had not yet been to college, but he was sweet, handsome, and quite a dreamer. He wanted to become a writer. I began to grow wary.

At that time, I was close to Rabbi Miller, who held me in high regard. Because he had heard Fredric March's wife, Florence Eldridge, give a reading of Ada Jackson's "Behold the Jew" on the radio, he invited me to give a performance for the sisterhood at the temple. So I began rehearsing the dramatization with organ music as background. In November, 1944, Rabbi Miller placed this announcement in *Temple Topics:*

Every lady in B'nai El is invited with her friends to one of the most outstanding and inspiring programs ever!

Monday, November 20th at the Sisterhood
Business meeting promptly at 1:00 o'clock, Program at 3:00

Dramatization by **Miss Ruth Kahn** of the prize winning English poem by **Ada Jackson**, *Behold the Jew* with **Mr. Howard Kelsey** at the organ.

Hear the "Eli Eli"—Rubenstein's "Melody in F" and many other familiar strains. Miss Florence Eldridge of stage and screen gave excerpts of this program on a national radio hookup recently—a program which was considered one of the best ever offered.

You cannot miss this!

Busy with rehearsals and studies, I had very full days and my love-life moved to the periphery.

One Sunday, during my architectural studies, my cousin Clarice and I attended a picnic given for Jewish soldiers. While I sat under a tree doing homework, Clarice chatted with Ralph Lynford, a soldier from New York stationed at Scott Field. They then corresponded while he was overseas. In 1945, after the end of World War II, Ralph came to St. Louis to propose. Clarice accepted his ring and asked me to be her maid of honor; Ralph invited his brother, Franklyn, to be his best man. The wedding was to take place at my parents' home during Thanksgiving weekend.

For the occasion, my parents invited Franklyn to be our houseguest. Upon hearing that the maid of honor was a student of architecture, he envisioned someone with horn-rimmed glasses, hair tied back in a bun, and unattractive, so he stayed in a hotel. When the Lynford family attended Thanksgiving dinner at our house, my mother whispered to my sister, Gloria, in the kitchen, "What do you think of Franklyn?" Gloria put her fingers to her nose, with "thumbs down" disapproval. Sometime during the day, Franklyn, who took a fancy to me, glanced at photos of Nathan and Irv on my dresser. From the hallway, I heard Clarice saying to him, "You haven't got a chance."

On Clarice's wedding day, Franklyn, wearing a morning suit, arrived in a limousine to pick me up for the bridal photographs. He looked elegant and seemed refined and gracious. We then stopped to get the bride and groom and went to have our pictures taken. On that day, we looked so happy with each other that everyone thought that our photograph was an engagement picture. At the wedding, Franklyn, not to be deterred, used his salesmanship and finesse on both my father and my father's sister, Alma, to convince them that I should visit New York during my Christmas holiday. Because I had never before been there, I saw an opportunity I could not miss. When Franklyn returned to New York, he wrote to me that he enjoyed the wedding and was "seriously considering reversing the cast."

After reading his letter, I knew I had to see Nathan, who at the time was in the hospital recovering from an appendectomy. I needed to decide whether to marry Nathan or Franklyn. Nathan, six years older, was uncertain about his career pursuit. Franklyn, the same age, had already established himself and invested as a junior partner in C.S. Brass Company. He was an outgoing, energetic entrepreneur. So, after talking with Nathan and

On Clarice's wedding day, Franklyn, wearing a morning suit, arrived in a limousine to pick up Ruth for the bridal photographs. He looked elegant and seemed refined and gracious. On that day, they looked so happy with each other that everyone thought that their photograph was an engagement picture.

feeling comfortable with Franklyn, I went to Lambert Airport to take my first airplane trip, an eight-and-a-half-hour flight, from St. Louis to New York City. Before my father put me on the plane, his parting words were: "Ruth, don't let any of those fast-talking New Yorkers sweep you off your feet!" And I replied, "Oh, Daddy!"

A week later, I was wearing a two carat diamond and platinum engagement ring. Franklyn or F.J. as he was known, sent a wire to my father that read, "I'd like to have your daughter's hand in marriage." Immediately, my father called on the telephone and told me, "We'll discuss the matter when you get home." I quickly called him back and said, "Dad, this is the man I'm going to marry." Because my family had met F.J. and his family at Clarice and Ralph's nuptials, by the time I got back to St. Louis, they had accepted him. Essentially, all that my father wanted was that I would complete my degree before I married. Upon my return, he asked, "When do we want to have the engagement party?" We decided to hold it in February.

On February 23, 1946, F.J. arrived at my parents' home carrying a New York confection, a Nesselrode pie. All evening, people raved about how good it was. One of my father's clients, Gene Schmidt from Boatmen's Bank, attended the event. During the festivity, F. J. somehow thought that Gene Schmidt was Dean Schmidt from the School of Architecture and talked with him about what a terrific student I had been. After the party, he realized his mistake and we all laughed about the confusion.

Because I knew that F.J.'s family would attend my graduation, I decided to combine the occasions and schedule the graduation and wedding two days apart. I ordered my satin wedding dress from Montaldo's and borrowed a magnificent antique Belgium lace tiara from May Kahn to be attached to my veil. For F.J. and me, June 15, 1946, was most memorable.

Opposite page, Top: Love note Ruth wrote to Franklyn. Bottom: Ruth and Franklyn with her parents, Dorothy and Adolph Kahn at Ruth's graduation

30 | My Life in Design

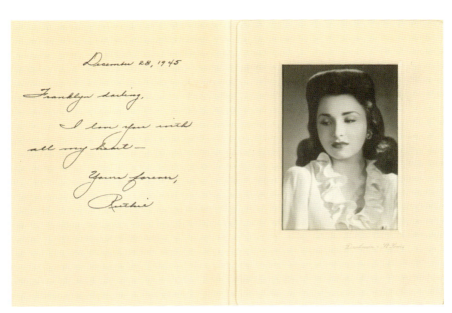

Form | 31

At the reception, F.J., knowing that I was a party-person who liked to stay until everybody was ready to leave, declared, "You're not going to be the last one here." That night, we escaped early to retire to the honeymoon suite. As planned, I graduated on Thursday, June 13 from Washington University and married on Saturday, June fifteenth at the Hotel Coronado. Within forty-eight hours, I went from cap and gown to bridal gown.

On Sunday morning, we headed for Lambert Airport, which in 1946 was one little building that looked like a cabin, and flew to Baltimore, Maryland, to spend our second night. On Monday morning, we boarded a seaplane for Bermuda. I wore a black cotton suit that was part of my trousseau. During the flight, we were seated with two other newly-married couples from New York and agreed to exchange hotel information once we landed.

After World War II, many of the hotels in Bermuda were not open, but through a travel agent, F.J. got us into The Princess, one of Bermuda's best. Because his name was Lynford and he had blond hair and blue eyes, F.J. had no problems. Once we landed in Bermuda, the two other couples, unhappy at their hotel, called us for assistance. We were unable to help them with their accommodations. Those were days of prejudice.

At the end of our two-week getaway, even though The Princess had a pool, we headed for the beach. The hotel prepared us a box lunch and provided transportation. Although the sun was not shining, we went swimming, ate our sandwiches, and returned. Somehow, during those few hours, my fair-skinned husband became severely burned. Red, rested, and radiant, we flew to New York the following morning. At twenty-one, I began a new life.

Above: On Sunday morning, Ruth and Franklyn headed for Lambert Airport, which in 1946 was one little building that looked like a cabin, and flew to Baltimore, Maryland, to spend their second night. Opposite page: Ruth in her wedding gown

"WHAT ARE
MY FUTURE
OPPORTUNITIES?"
I ASKED.

Chapter Two: Unity and Variety

Our happy landing was at Long Beach, New York, a strip along the Atlantic Ocean, where we stayed at a hotel until our Flushing apartment was ready. Each morning, F.J. commuted about an hour to work in Manhattan. For a month, I splashed at the seashore and watched women in their mink stoles strut the boardwalk in the one-hundred-degree weather. It was such an amusing sight for someone from St. Louis to witness.

A year later, my parents traveled by train from St. Louis to visit us. They mentioned that a client of my father's and his wife were going to stop by New York, after seeing their son at Amherst. F.J. suggested that we all have lunch in Manhattan at Hampshire House on Central Park South. It had an open courtyard and delicious food, so we invited them to meet us there. On that warm October day, I donned my new brown Alaskan seal coat that my sister-in-law, also named Ruth Lynford, had convinced F.J. to purchase. Young and naïve, I showed off the coat.

As soon as I set foot in New York, I wanted to work. On our honeymoon, I spoke with F.J. about my career desires. Although he seemed a bit disappointed, he did not say anything. During the 1940s, most people assumed that women stayed at home and took care of the house. But F.J. was secure and did not accept the perception that if a woman worked, it showed a man's inability to support her.

My first job was at York & Sawyer, a prestigious architectural firm in Manhattan, no longer in existence. I did drafting or "pushing a pencil," as it was called. They told me that my performance was very good. But after three years, I asked, "What are my future opportunities?" One of the principals responded, "Frankly, Ruth, we do not allow women out in the field or in the design studio."

After World War II, there was a tremendous amount of new construction and architects were overwhelmed with designs for the shells of apartments and office buildings. The interior spaces, concrete floors, and concrete ceilings, presented an invitation for interior designers to step in and complete them. Those spaces offered the niche for interior design to begin its coming-of-age.

When an ad appeared in *The New York Times* seeking an interior designer to open a design department in an antique shop, I answered it. Those were the days when an applicant carried a case, a large, black leather portfolio, to the interview.

Eager to design, I left York & Sawyer and began work as a freelancer. I worked on offices for the Schubert family at the Schubert Theater and other commercial and residential projects. When an ad appeared in *The New York Times* seeking an interior designer to open a design department in an antique shop, I answered it. Those were the days when an applicant carried a portfolio, a large black leather case, to the interview. At about five-thirty one evening I arrived at the North Shore Gallery to find a long line of thirty-two people. I was one of the last to be interviewed and did not think I had a chance. The next morning, however, I received a telephone call informing me that the job was mine. When I told the owner, "I will be available in two weeks," he said, "Fine."

The problem was that I had not really done enough interior design work in New York to know the wholesale sources for everything that went into interiors: where to go to buy furniture, fabrics, carpeting, wall covering, lighting, and accessories. So during those fourteen days, I bustled about acquainting myself with all the suppliers, a kind of crash course or independent study.

At the North Shore Gallery, I did mostly residential interior design projects with many upscale clients. The owner encouraged me to use the antiques in the shop, but I was free, as well, to find everything else on the open market. I relished my life.

F.J. then decided to purchase Dumont Coal and Lumber in Dumont, New Jersey. Unbeknownst to him, he or someone in the firm had to be a licensed Weighmaster, to weigh the tonnage of coal. We then quickly moved to New Jersey and became residents.

I gave up my North Shore Gallery job, and F.J., our baby, Jeffrey, and I settled in a new five-room, garden apartment that still had mud on the driveway. F.J. continued in his position as junior partner at C.S. Brass

Previous page:
Ruth and F.J. in Spain, 1966

Company in Manhattan, which he did not want to leave for a year, so that he could receive his annual bonus. To assist him in Dumont, he invited Nathan Davis, a college chum, to be his partner. Needing additional help, F.J. asked Ralph, one of his older brothers, to work with Nathan while he completed the year in Manhattan. While Nathan Davis and Ralph Lynford were running the business, they wanted me to join them, which I did. At Dumont Coal and Lumber, I was able to see exactly how wood and materials were cut. After one year, F.J. returned to Dumont and soon discovered that he and I could not work well together; both egos were just too strong. I decided to leave the business.

At the time, Gloria, my sister, needed my help in planning her wedding to Raymond Solomon at the Colony Club, so I flew to St. Louis with Jeffrey. There, Gloria and I selected everything: her dress, bridesmaids' dresses, flowers, and cake. Together, we coordinated the details.

While I was away, F.J. noticed a small building for rent on Kinderkamack Road in Oradell, New Jersey, and took it upon himself to lease it for me to start my own venture. When I returned, there it was. F.J. told me, "I will subsidize you for three years; then you are on your own."

We fixed up the tiny shop and put up a sign that read "R.K. Lynford & Co." At twenty-five years of age, I did not want people to know that I was young and a woman. A year later, I had outgrown the building and planned to move. When I mentioned to Clotilda Demarest, the owner, that I needed to relocate, she responded, "Oh, no! I'll build a new building onto the existing one, so that you'll have enough space." I said, "Perfect."

In the addition, I had lovely furniture on consignment and a large counter that held wallpaper books and all other interior products. I displayed tables and chairs in the expansive, floor-to-ceiling windows that faced Kinderkamack Road. I then took on an assistant and expanded the enterprise, which, at that time was solely interior design.

Still occupying our small apartment in Dumont, F.J. and I decided that we needed a home. One day, we saw an ad in *The New York Times* listing a ten-room house for sale in Ho-Ho-Kus, New Jersey, at 35 Lloyd Road. While we were in our car viewing the property, he announced, "That's the house we're buying," and we did. F.J. made decisions quickly, not hurriedly, but always with good thought. It was a modern, four-bedroom residence with huge, glass windows, and a screened-in porch designed by an architect. My mother, excited about our additional space, said, "Ruth, you have to have more than one child." We moved to Ho-Ho-Kus with one child; ten years later we moved out with four—Jeffrey, Lance, Leslye, our daughter, and Lloyd. All four were born in Doctors Hospital across from Gracie Mansion. My mother then quipped, "I didn't mean to oversell the idea."

Because F.J. and I both worked full-time, we employed live-in help. F.J. needed assistance in the lumberyard, as well, so we took in international couples who wanted to spend time in the New York area for several years, earn money, and then go back to their native countries. They resided in our lower level suite which had its own entrance.

The first couple we hired was French. The husband drove our car back and forth to the lumberyard; the wife was our housekeeper and a gifted piano player, who gave Jeffrey lessons. Each night we four adults shared a jug of wine at our dinners.

During the Ho-Ho-Kus years, we entertained, hosting many grand functions. As a party-person, I designed the invitations, menus, and place cards and selected the seating arrangements and table accoutrements. Then, with gusto, I took part in the merry-making with family, friends, and business customers. It was the planning, as well as the parties, that I savored.

When the French couple returned to France, we hired Joanna and Len, who were Dutch. While they were with us, F.J. and I had the opportunity to go abroad for six weeks on a tour organized by the American Society of Interior Designers for only eight hundred sixty-five dollars per person. For support, I asked my mother to come and stay with Joanna, Len, and the children. F.J. and I then traveled to Europe by ship on the S.S. *Olympia,* a Greek ocean liner. Our first stop was Portugal, where the boat docked parallel to the shore. From there, we went by train to Italy.

When our group of about six hundred arrived in Venice, we were invited as guests to a gala given by the owner of the Fortuny empire. Dressed in black-tie attire, we were picked up by boat and taken to the owner's

Opposite page: Ruth and F.J. fixed up the tiny shop and put up a sign that read, "R.K. Lynford & Co." At twenty-five years of age, Ruth did not want people to know that she was young and a woman.

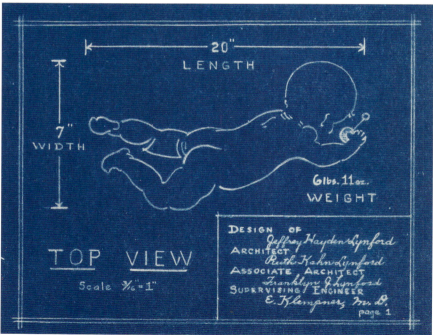

home on an island about a half-hour from Venice. During the visit, we were shown through the Fortuny Factory, known for its secret formula for making and printing incredible fabrics. We then entered her grounds, lit by dazzling, outdoor lanterns hanging everywhere. In long dresses and tuxedos, we roamed through the mansion, where we were served a sumptuous dinner, followed by violin music. Several hours later, we boarded a boat back to Venice. It was absolutely the most magnificent party I had ever experienced. A year later, Fortuny named one of its fabrics "Olympia" after the ship that carried us across the water.

From Italy, we continued on to France and England. While vacationing, F.J. and I received a letter from Jeffrey, saying that his brother, Lance, had come to think of Joanna as his mother. During our return passage on the *Queen Elizabeth*, I was often seasick and frequently stayed in the stateroom; F.J., however, never missed a meal. Much to our delight, back in Ho-Ho-Kus, we learned that I was pregnant with Lloyd, our youngest.

Over the years, our Ho-Ho-Kus house had become too small. It was tight with two children in each bedroom, so I began drawing plans to add an extension, using lumber and building supplies from Dumont Coal and Lumber. When we figured out the cost of the materials, the contractor, and the like, we determined that the expense out-priced the neighborhood. We then put our house on the market and considered building a place on two acres of land that we owned in Saddle River, New Jersey.

At the time, some old homes in Tuxedo Park and Rockland County in New York State became available. So, one Sunday, F.J. and I answered an ad. A lovely realtor took us to Tuxedo Park known then for its gorgeous homes, but with high taxes. She then said, "I have a house in West Nyack, where the taxes are not extreme, that I would like for you to see." It was an historic landmark

Above: Ruth's family in their Ho-Ho-Kus home. Ruth always dressed her children in the same fabrics. The eldest, Jeffrey, asked, "Mother why are we dressed in pajamas in the middle of the day?" Opposite page: Birth announcement for Ruth's son, Jeffrey

Unity and Variety | 43

in Rockland County rumored to have been the campsite of George Washington and his troops in 1780, but was definitely the site of the last witch trial, which took place in the State of New York, in 1816. The twenty-two-room residence with five fireplaces sat on almost four acres of wooded grounds. It included a lake, a waterfall, two bridges, a spring, an old grist mill, walking paths, and a stone wall.

We walked up the steps and peered into the windows, which were spectacular French doors. We saw the French parquet floors, and the *trumeau* on the fireplace and panels above the doorways done by sculptor Louis Richard, a former owner of the property. F.J. and I both said, "If the rest of the house is anything like this, we are going to buy it." In that way, he and I were in complete accord. We liked the same homes, as long as we could afford them.

We bought the house in 1960, for fifty thousand dollars, and moved in at the end of August, the same year that Jeffrey was having his bar mitzvah at a congregation in Fair Lawn, New Jersey. Our goal was to get the whole interior repainted, ready for the bar mitzvah luncheon.

We certainly did not have sufficient furniture to fill all of the rooms, but we had enough to make do. For a house gift, my parents sent a fifteen-hundred-dollar check for dining room furniture. I found an antique French Empire, round, walnut table with many leaves and used the check for that. When my parents came to visit, they liked the table, but saw no chairs, no buffet, or anything else. My mother, extremely disappointed, asked, "Where is the rest of the furniture? Fifteen-hundred-dollars and all you got was a table?" I reassured her saying, "I have a table that I truly, truly, love." Fortunately, I then remembered that when I designed the interior of singer Kitty Kallen's home in Englewood, New Jersey, I had purchased six, simple, good-looking, Victorian chairs,

Opposite page: West Nyack house. The twenty-two-room residence with five fireplaces sat on almost four acres of wooded grounds. It included a lake, a waterfall, two bridges, a spring, an old grist mill, walking paths, and a stone wall.

Unity and Variety | 45

with black-and-white houndstooth check fabric seats, that were of no use to her. I unpacked them and set them around our dining room table. Over the years, in keeping with the house, I furnished nearly the entire place with American, French, and English antiques.

Our idyllic, white brick, sandstone, and stucco three-story home located at 135 Strawtown Road appeared to be a bit of a conglomeration. Some of it was pre-Revolutionary with very thick walls; the front was more classical with columns. Nonetheless, it rested comfortably on uneven land, on a corner piece of property with two circular driveways.

The first floor had an entrance hall, a front and back staircase, a huge living room, and a large dining room, each with a fireplace and French doors leading to a wooden porch with an antique brick floor, a den, a kitchen, a butler's pantry, a powder room, and a glass-enclosed solarium with window seats and a beamed ceiling. In addition, it had another suite of rooms, one of which I turned into my office, with an adjacent kitchen and bath.

The office ceiling consisted of Upson board, a kind of fiberboard, in disrepair. I planned to ask F.J. to send lumber, so that I could put up some false beams. One day, I invited our neighbor Mr. Nicholson, a carpenter, to stop by and told him what I wanted to do with the ceiling. Looking up, he said, "You know, Mrs. Lynford, when I was a little boy, the Richards lived here. I think I remember a beautiful, beamed ceiling underneath this." We then removed the Upson board and, sure enough, a magnificent, octagon, oak ceiling appeared.

Our large, glass solarium also had an amazing, wood-beamed ceiling and pine flooring. We were told that, at one time, the ceiling had been glass, but apparently during a fire in the 1890s, a firefighter fell through the roof. So, when it was rebuilt, the owner replaced the glass with wood.

Opposite page: West Nyack house. Ruth's idyllic white brick, sandstone, and stucco three-story home located at 135 Strawtown Road appeared to be a bit of a conglomeration. Some of it was pre-Revolutionary with very thick walls. All of the fixtures and some of the furnishings were antiques. The fixtures in the living room were from a trip to Venice.

The second floor contained a study, a four-and-a-half-room apartment with a separate entrance, originally known as "the slave quarters," a master bedroom suite with a fireplace, and four additional bedrooms. One bedroom we gave to Jeffrey, one to Leslye, and the largest one with the windows on three sides to Lance and Lloyd. The extra bedroom was for guests. There was also a third floor which had three bedrooms, a bath, a game room, and a huge clothes closet.

One Sunday morning, shortly after we moved in, F.J. and I heard a knock on our bedroom door and in walked Lloyd, all of four years old, with arms crossed. He said, "Mother, I've had it with Lance!" I responded, "Okay, Lloyd, you move into the guest room." An hour later, I woke up and saw that he had carried everything of his into the guest room and never moved back. From that day on, each child occupied a private room.

My sister, Gloria, was a frequent guest at West Nyack. At twenty-nine, she became a widow when Raymond, her husband, was killed in a plane crash. Fortunately, she not only had a degree in social work, but also had begun law school. Taller than I, Gloria sported big, brown eyes and dark skin. She was stunning. On her visits from Chicago, she often brought gentlemen who wished to marry her because they knew that she had inherited a great sum of money. We voted "thumbs down" on most of them. F.J. then acted on an idea and introduced Gloria to Norman Prisament, a divorced brother of one of our best friends. He was a match, so, in 1964, their wedding took place in our home. Norman adopted Gloria's two sons, Marc and Lee, from her first marriage. Together, they had another son, Robert. The five Prisaments lived nearby in Dobbs Ferry, New York.

Not long after Gloria's arrival, my father and mother decided to pull up their Missouri roots, move to West Nyack, and join us. My father sold his accounting practice.

Opposite page: Ruth's large glass solarium also had an amazing, wood-beamed ceiling and pine flooring. They were told that at one time the ceiling had been glass, but apparently during a fire in the 1890s, a firefighter fell through the roof. So when it was rebuilt, the owner replaced the glass with wood. The sixty-inch round, drop-leaf, light walnut, antique English table now sits in Ruth's living room.

With Gloria's financial help, I redesigned the apartment that had once been "the slave quarters." My parents then shipped their furniture, carpet, and accessories that I had supplied in St. Louis. After the floor covering was installed and the furniture was arranged, we held a ribbon-cutting ceremony to herald their arrival. They enjoyed their combination living-dining room, kitchen and breakfast area, bedroom, and another room, with a private entrance, that became my father's office. Never one to sit still, my father found a job as an accounting professor in White Plains. Transplanted, my parents were ecstatic having their two daughters, two sons-in-law, and seven grandchildren nearby. Their move worked out nicely for all of us.

As the children grew older, F.J. and I no longer needed live-in couples; instead, Janie, our devoted housekeeper from Ho-Ho-Kus, lived with us. Janie literally raised our children; she was their surrogate mother. On weekends, when she was off, my parents joined us for Sunday dinner in the solarium. My mother, who liked to cook and bake, brought her leftovers, and I pulled out mine. We combined the fare. Together, the eight of us sat at the large round table and ate potluck. We had no automatic dishwasher, so I used paper plates, cups, and napkins. My husband, however, preferred china plates, glassware, and silverware. So, my parents, the four children, and I used paper; F.J. used china. That became our Sunday ritual.

In those years, I continued to juggle home and work. I was able to have an office on the premises and an assistant who came in on weekdays. We were also blessed with Janie, who did the cooking Monday through Friday. When F.J. wanted to entertain, I hosted Saturday night black-tie dinner parties. Although I took French cooking lessons in the neighborhood, they were a waste of time. The children had no interest in cuisine. The first

Opposite page: At the Lynford household, they were interested in animals. From a very young age, Lance, their second son, always wanted a dog. Finally, for his ninth birthday, F.J. and Ruth decided to surprise him with a puppy from one of her suppliers in Manhattan who bred miniature schnauzers. Duke sits in the boat and on the lawn with the children.

recipe I learned to prepare was filet of sole Veronique, that is, with grapes. Jeffrey, Lesyle, Lance, and Lloyd wanted nothing to do with it; they liked Janie's fried chicken.

Routinely, each Saturday I made a grocery list and the five of us did the weekly marketing. Jeffrey, Lance, and Lloyd were in charge of the paper goods; they tossed toilet tissue and paper towels to each other from one end of the aisle to the other. Leslye went for the produce; I took care of all the protein—meat, fish, and the like. Within minutes, shopping turned into frivolity. One time when I was in the hospital briefly, F.J. took the children marketing. Observing their antics and the accompanying hilarity, he warned, "I will give you fifteen minutes." He never forgot their exuberance.

Ruth and F.J., 1979

In our household, we all were interested in animals. From a very young age, Lance always wanted a dog. Finally, for his ninth birthday, F.J. and I decided to surprise him with a puppy from one of my suppliers in Manhattan who bred miniature schnauzers. F.J. was not much of a dog lover, but he went along with me to look at the litter. Beforehand, we agreed to stand apart if he did not want a puppy, and stand together if he did. Well, when F.J. saw the adorable, little, six-week-old schnauzer, we took him home in a box. Leslye was so afraid of dogs that when she saw the bounding bundle, she stood on a chair. Years later, that dog, eventually named "Duke," slept on her bed.

When Gloria met Duke, she, too, wanted to buy a miniature schnauzer, which she did, and called him "Whiskers." Some people say that canines take on the personality and behavior of their owners. My father tended to agree, as he tried patiently to teach Duke and Whiskers the standard commands: "come," "stay," "sit," "speak," and "heel." In time, Lance's dog became an integral part of the Lynford family. When our family and Gloria's family traveled together to Washington, D.C., Duke, a barker like other schnauzers, often escorted us.

With offices in Manhattan, F.J. and I also kept a pied-à-terre there. At first, it was a small one, but as the children grew older, they preferred the city and not everyone could go. We then devised a competition: whoever had the neatest room, could have a weekend in the city. Lance, the tidiest, always won. Duke obediently came along. Interestingly, the Manhattan atmosphere depressed Duke, who lay listless on the floor. When we returned to West Nyack, however, he was the happiest, prancing dog ever imagined. Later, when we acquired a larger apartment with several bedrooms, all of us could be together in the city and enjoy the hubbub.

During our marriage, F.J. and I, who loved to travel, took many trips without the children, most frequently to France and Mexico. Often we went with groups organized by the American Society of Interior Designers; other times we traveled on our own. After our initial European adventure and a trip to Madrid, many others followed: Spain, Denmark, Sweden, Russia, Portugal, Israel, Italy, Greece, and Hungary. Ever interested in the sights, countryside, museums, artifacts, food, and entertainment, we found that ultimately, it was the people we met who gave meaning to our travel.

A second trip to Spain took us to Barcelona to visit Lloyd, while he was experiencing the St. Paul's Prep School year abroad. His host family, of Catalan descent, spoke no English. We spoke no Spanish, but we seemed to get along very well. The lady of the house told me that when Lloyd first arrived, she was very upset with him, because he always made his bed before he left for school. She emphasized that it was her responsibility, not his. Smiling, I then told her, "You are influencing my son. When he returns home, he'll be spoiled." After Lloyd showed us around Barcelona, F.J. and I then took a boat, passed the Strait of Gibraltar, and went on to wandering the bazaar stalls, bartering with the vendors, and reveling in the fascinations of Morocco.

In Copenhagen, it was a jeweler who sized a gold pinky ring with diamonds that F.J. purchased for me, who stayed in our memories. As we hastily boarded a plane for Sweden, the jeweler dashed to the airport loading area to meet us. He said, "I have your ring." F.J. responded, "I don't have time to pay you." The gentleman continued, "That's perfectly all right. You take the ring, and I'm trusting you'll send me a check."

On a conference trip to St. Petersburg, Russia, we were taken on an excursion outside of town to the breathtaking Catherine Palace, to see the incredible restoration. After we witnessed the gilt and grandeur of about a half-dozen rooms, the guide said, "I'm sorry, but the next room isn't completed." When we pleaded with him to show us anyway, he agreed. We walked in. On the ceiling there was splendor— amethyst

Unity and Variety | 53

hanging crystal chandeliers. A man with a beret stood on a ladder doing some of the repair work. Collectively, we sighed, "Aah." The Russian on the ladder suddenly burst into tears. When we asked the guide why he was crying, he said that the gentleman was so touched by the "oohs" and "aahs" over his eleven-year labor, that the tears just rolled down his face.

F.J. and I also took a trip on our own to Hungary, the birthplace of his father, Herman, which, too, proved to be revealing. After checking into a fine hotel and having dinner, F.J. told the maitre d,' "We'd like to order Palacsintas for breakfast," a pastry similar to a crepe, filled with apricot jam and topped with powdered sugar, that his mother, Rose, made on Sunday mornings for our children. Respectfully, the maitre d' made note of F.J.'s request, but looked at him a bit strangely. When we came down for breakfast the following morning, a waiter carried in a huge, silver platter with long, narrowing points, covered by an elaborate dome. He removed the dome and there were the Palacsintas, swimming in chocolate sauce and nuts. That morning, with chocolate on our lips, we learned that in Hungary, the Hungarians have Palacsintas for dessert, and usually in the evening. From that day on, we laughed at the Lynford family variant of a Hungarian tradition.

For my fiftieth birthday, F.J. was caught up with business, so I decided to go with a small group of about twenty designers and architects on a conference trip to India. We flew nonstop from New York to Mumbai and then had a short ride to New Delhi where we stayed in a top-quality Oberoi Hotel. On the first night, we were invited to a barbecue at the home of a young, wealthy, newly-married, Indian woman, an Oberoi, who looked very much like Elizabeth Taylor. Her home was designed by an Indian architect who had studied in America. Just by chance, I happened to ask the concierge, "What do I wear

Opposite page: Photos from Lloyd's bar mitzvah celebration at Ruth's home. Over the years, the house in West Nyack was a scene of lively parties, occasions, and events: Jeff's bar mitzvah, Lance's confirmation, Lloyd's bar mitzvah, Gloria's wedding, birthday celebrations, and holiday gatherings.

> The house had many lives. It held ours for nearly twenty years. For me, those were years of wonder.

to an Indian barbecue?" He said, "Oh, Mrs. Lynford, this is a very elegant affair in India, especially at the estate. You wear your finest clothes." Luckily, I had packed a pair of silver satin, wide pants that looked like a skirt and a silver lamé, sleeveless top, so I was ready to go. As we arrived by bus, we saw a huge pig on a spit, rotating in a pit. We then sat down to a formal dinner, complete with silver service, china, and big silver platters with silver domes. Afterwards, the young architect who designed the home, as well as a private home on the grounds, took me on a tour of the property. It was a splendid evening, grand in every way.

Our group then traveled to Agra, where we saw the Taj Mahal in moonlight, and moved on to Dal Lake where I lived on a houseboat in Srinagar for a week. After that, we went to the rug factories, where we watched eight-year-olds sitting at looms, weaving intricate wool carpets, dipping them into the river, and then placing them on the banks to dry. The trip to India was a fiftieth birthday gift beyond worth.

From our travels, F.J. and I returned to our family renewed, inspired, and awakened. West Nyack, unfailingly, provided a welcoming respite. For us, it was always, "Home, Sweet Home."

Over the years, our house in West Nyack was a scene of lively parties, occasions, and events: Jeff's bar mitzvah, Lance's confirmation, Lloyd's bar mitzvah, Gloria's wedding, birthday celebrations, and holiday gatherings. During the winter, the children skated on the pond and then came indoors for hot chocolate and toasted marshmallows. During the summer, they enjoyed romping on the grounds and rowing in our little "dinghy" boat. The seasons marked the day-to-day moments and rites of passage alike.

Our West Nyack home was a piece of a dream. We loved it. Finally, in 1979, the four children, who had gone

56 | My Life in Design

off to or finished college, no longer seemed interested in owning the property. With just the two of us, F.J. and I decided to leave, but not before we gave a farewell party for our haven.

The house had many lives. It held ours for nearly twenty years. For me, those were years of wonder.

"DESIGNING SPARKED MY IMAGINATION."

Chapter Three: Light

When F.J. and I sold our West Nyack home, we were able to purchase three abodes: a small apartment on Fifth Avenue, a charming little country house in Somers, New York, and a large apartment in Palm Beach, Florida. Extending the bright memories of West Nyack, we dispersed the furniture and art among our three places and four children. All the while, my offices in Manhattan and Palm Beach flourished.

At the Manhattan office, located at 225 East 57th Street, I initially shared space with Lloyd Bell, an interior designer. Although we created separate quarters, the area eventually became too small for both of us. As the last one in, I felt obligated to move.

I then acquired another office in the same building. Sanna Mayo, Victor Borge's eldest daughter, had worked for me, and returned after giving birth to her second daughter, Lucy. Fluent in French and a fine writer, Sanna proved invaluable, helping me with my many speeches on the physical and psychological effects of the built environment. One morning, I said, "Sanna, I'd like for you to become a partner." The timing was perfect. In 1976, we became Lynford Mayo Associates, Inc. With a degree in architecture, I was interested in space; Sanna had a flair for color, fabrics, and wallcoverings. Together, we made a fine professional duo.

When the largest designer's office-apartment became available in the building, we moved in. During those days, the owner had difficulty renting the units, so he sought out interior designers, with the condition that they furnish the residential apartments with sleep sofas or create a bedroom to prove that they were occupying the spaces as residences. The developer was the same person who did the Design Building on Third Avenue.

In our fourteenth-floor office, Sanna and I created an attractive, well-organized setting. We then hosted an opening, commemorating the beginning of Lynford Mayo Associates, Inc. Sanna Sarabel Borge, Sanna's mother, and Lester Dundes, the publisher of *Interior Design* were among those who attended the gala.

At the time, most of our design work occurred in Manhattan, but I also had an office in Palm Beach, Florida. During the 1970s, Palm Beach boomed along the ocean front. F.J. loved it there. He craved the warmth of "The Sunshine State," so much so, that we became Florida residents, spending six months and a day in the South, and the remaining months in the North. Our first Florida apartment, a rental on the fifth floor of a building on State Route A1A, looked out on a spectacular Atlantic Ocean view. Everything was luminous.

The Palm Beach office was located in the Armour Building at 205 Worth Avenue next to Eugene Lawrence, an architect who worked with Sandy Weinstock, a Palm Beach developer. When Weinstock heard that I had a degree in architecture, even though he had already hired Lawrence, he asked if I would also be interested in assisting him with Beach Point, a project which included three apartment buildings and a clubhouse right on the water. I accepted.

At the time, Steven Louie, a talented designer and one of my so-called "designing children," moonlighted for me in New York. Born in Brooklyn to Chinese parents, Steve exhibited design genius. When Weinstock asked me to help him with Beach Point, I sat down with Steve and said, "I'd like us to present three drawings for the buildings to be called Beach Point." Shortly after, he brought me a sketch of three structures, all rectangular. I knew that what Weinstock wanted was nonlinear buildings, so I told Steve, "Please sketch a building with curved corners." That afternoon, he left my Manhattan office, and drew one overnight. The following morning, I flew to Palm Beach carrying the three, rectangular sketches and the curved one. I showed Weinstock the drawings. When he saw the curved sketch, he said, "That's it. That's the one!"

F.J. and I then decided to purchase a Beach Point apartment. We chose one on the top floor, the sixth, with a wrap-around terrace facing the Atlantic Ocean. In our large, two-bedroom unit, I put in beige, travertine marble floors, lacquered-wood furniture, many built-ins,

Above: Ruth wanted to present three drawings for the buildings to be called Beach Point. Shortly after she asked Steve for sketches, he brought her a sketch of three structures, all rectangular. She knew that what Weinstock wanted was nonlinear buildings, so she told Steve, "Please sketch a building with curved corners."
Opposite page: An interior for one of the Beach Point clients

Previous page: Ruth and Sanna in their office

and incredible lighting. On the marble floor in our entry, I placed a tomato-red, nine-by-twelve-foot, antique Heriz Persian carpet. Everything offered the lightness of living.

Besides designing the Beach Point buildings and the interiors of many of the apartments, we did all the lobby spaces. In keeping with the outdoor setting, we covered the interior walls with natural sisal. Of course, in such a big project, it was impossible to please every buyer or owner. Some residents liked the wall covering; others did not. F.J. finally said, "Ruth, from now on, please do not ever design the public space of a building in which we live."

All in all, F.J. and I stepped in at the beginning of Beach Point and we loved it. From dawn to dusk, we were surrounded by beauty. On a clear day, we could see the ships dotting the Atlantic. In 1995, when F.J. passed away, I felt it was time to sell the apartment and all of its furnishings. Above all other projects, Beach Point shines as a personal and professional highlight; we did the whole thing, inside and out.

A favorite residential project was in Pound Ridge, New York, at 264 Trinity Pass Road. Joan Throckmorton and Sheldon Satin, a married couple, were our clients. Originally, it was a speculative, weekend house, but they decided to extend the whole place and make it into their permanent home and offices. Although I designed the exterior and interior, the architect of the original residence served as the architect of record for the expansion. Bryan English, another one of my "designing children," became my project colleague.

Shelly and Joan both worked in public relations, but in different aspects of it. Married before, Shelly had adult children. He was short, Jewish, and originally from Brooklyn. In contrast, Joan was a tall, slender, and distinguished-looking woman from New England, who

Opposite page: Living Room at Pound Ridge home. A favorite residential project of Ruth's was in Pound Ridge, New York, at 264 Trinity Pass Road. Joan Throckmorton and Sheldon Satin, a married couple, were her clients.

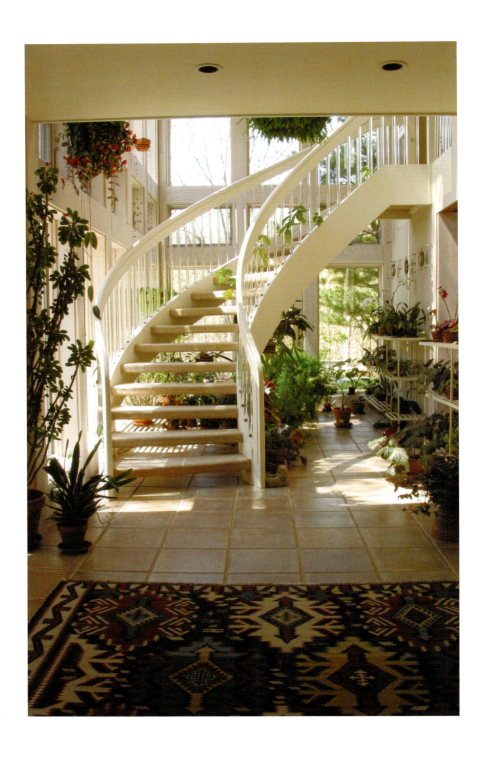

reminded me so much of Katharine Hepburn. On weekends, they held performances in their home; Shelly sang and, afterwards, Joan served a buffet. While working with them, I could tell that they were very much in love.

When I approached this project, or any project, the first thing I did was talk with the clients about their needs and goals. I also explored things about their pasts, how they lived in the present, and how they envisioned the future. At times, I had to read between the lines by listening to their words and then observing their daily lives. Often, I gleaned ideas from nonverbal cues. A shake or turn of the head, a smile or frown, a closed or open hand, a shrug of the shoulders, or a flick, squint, or roll of the eyes offered insight. I tried to get to know them, in hopes that the design could capture their personalities.

After making a list of the various needs and requirements, I developed two or three possibilities. All of this, of course, was far in advance of any deep consideration of aesthetics. So, I took it one step at a time, building on decisions. My eyes were on the clients and my ears were open to them.

Usually, I provided two schemes. At the onset, I introduced the concept that I found to be preferable; I showed the second one only if they had a problem with the first. Together, we came to a decision. Design is always about mutual problem solving.

I then prepared elevations showing the layout of the walls, furniture, and lighting, and talked about color and textiles to determine the clients' reactions, their likes and dislikes. I asked questions such as: "What are your favorite colors? What colors do you dislike? How do you respond to different kinds of patterns?" After we carefully listened to the client responses, we were ready to go. Only then could we begin the search for fabrics, carpets, wall coverings, paint, plumbing, or lighting fixtures.

Opposite page: The Pound Ridge couple's extension included a staircase. Ruth preferred a curved, sweeping one, which was successfully put in. Generous, and desiring only the best, Shelly was willing to pay more. Joan was a bit more frugal.

The most difficult kind of designing was when there was no personality to design for, as in a model home or display. I then tried to choose a theme. Each project, of any kind, always presents a new problem, fresh and challenging.

The Pound Ridge couple's extension included a staircase. I preferred a curved, sweeping one, which we successfully put in. Generous, and desiring only the best, Shelly was willing to pay more. Joan was a bit more frugal.

For the Pound Ridge effort, even though the couple's spending habits differed, their tastes were identical. Ultimately, we brought the budget and tastes together and had the pleasure of satisfying their design preferences. The result proved to be both inviting and functional, large enough to arrange chairs auditorium-style for Shelly's performances, and fitting for Joan to serve comfortably throughout the living/dining area.

Over time, Bryan and I became very involved in Shelly and Joan's lives. We saw how they lived their days. We knew much about each of them by working closely with the twosome for so long. At completion, the new extension captured their glow.

Another illuminating residential design project was with the Roberts family. It began with a bit of decorating in their modest, two-story house in Rockland County. The Roberts, their three children, and pets then moved into an eleven-room, pre-Civil War farmhouse, surrounded by acreage, in New Hempstead, New York. It had great potential and they wanted to make it their own. From the beginning, they envisioned a comfortable, efficient kitchen and a cozy, adjoining family room. Together, in keeping with the rich history of the home, we mapped out a plan. We knocked out an adjacent wall to the kitchen and added a new room with a slanted roof, beams and skylights on the ceiling, and barn-siding on

Opposite page: Andrea Roberts's dining room in Piermont. All the furnishings were from the New Hempstead farmhouse.

68 | My Life in Design

the walls. When completed, this project radiated light and warmth.

Some time later, I received a call from Andrea Roberts telling me that she had divorced and married Louis Pertschuk, a physician, and they wanted me to help them with the New Hempstead house. We first worked on the dining room and then on the small living room, large enough for two love seats. Eventually, we made changes in the entire house. When the children moved out, Andrea, a psychologist, considered making the home larger by putting on a third floor, but, ultimately, she and Lou decided to sell it.

They then purchased a lovely, attached home with three levels overlooking the Hudson River in Piermont, New Jersey. We designed the interiors from the ground up. On the lower level, we partitioned the two-car garage, where Andrea's office is, so that her clients could come in without having to wander through the ground floor. From the lower level, a flight of stairs leads to a living room, dining room, family room, kitchen, breakfast area, and powder room. On the second floor, there is a guest room and master bedroom, each with an en suite bath.

In this project, a challenge was to take furnishings that were in a rustic setting and make them work in a more sophisticated one. Andrea is a traditionalist. Her dining room chairs are French, the table is Louis XV, and everything is blue and white. Our only purchase was a square coffee table with a glass top and iron base to put between the two love seats in the living room. In her second-floor guest room, we placed a colorful Turkish rug that she and her now late husband Lou brought back from a vacation. I am most pleased that all of the furniture, rugs, and lamps from New Hempstead were used in Piermont. Everything found a place. Most importantly, Andrea is

Opposite page: The large living room opened up the downstairs. Under the staircase, Ruth designed an off-white lacquer cabinet that could act as a buffet. It came all the way around into the living room where she had a black leather, three-piece sofa cut to fit into the corner. Over it, she hung an abstract painting by Joan Mitchell. Accented by a rug in white, black, and gray, the setting was striking.

Light | 71

delightfully happy there. Interestingly, through the design process, we have cultivated a personal, long-term relationship.

Another project particularly dear to me, was for my late, younger sister Gloria's home in Hastings-on-Hudson, New York. Gloria always loved modern design; she liked things sleek. After the death of her first husband, I had the pleasure of doing the interior of her Chicago apartment. Over the years, she left social work, finished her law degree, and worked as a litigator until she took an acting course, which led her to the stage and screen to be cast in Arthur Miller's Broadway production of *A View from the Bridge*, and in the television miniseries, "Angels in America."

In the interim, I helped her and Norman Prisament, her second husband, with their Dobbs Ferry home, a new, classic dwelling with columns painted white. For the sake of compromise, I divided the rooms of that house according to their individual design preferences. The dining room was traditional with Louis XV chairs, table, and a crystal chandelier which pleased Norman. The master bedroom furnishings tilted more to the modern, which delighted Gloria. The living room was eclectic; parts of it satisfied each of them. After Norman passed away and her three sons were grown, Gloria decided to sell the house.

She located a light, airy, two-floor, corner unit in a gated golf club community in Hastings-on-Hudson. Most likely a sales model, it was one of the last units available. It appealed to her. Although there were two interior architectural features that she was not happy with—a colonial fireplace and a wooden spindle handrail from first to second floor—this house included a master bedroom, a large dressing room, a bathroom, and a closet containing a washer and dryer on the first floor. So, ultimately, all of her living could take place on one floor.

Opposite page: On the first floor, the overall color scheme of white, gray, and black helped the artwork stand out. For the dining room, Ruth bought Italian-made furniture designed by Massimo and Lella Vignelli, two famous Italian architects residing in New York. With elegance it sat on light, oak floors. A Roy Lichtenstein painting graced one wall, two Robert Motherwells, another.

Above: Ruth and her sister Gloria. This project was uniquely wonderful. From Ruth's years of living with Gloria and traveling with her to Egypt and Japan, Ruth knew her sister and her tastes. As with other projects, Ruth presented the drawings and photographs of furniture for her approval. Unlike other projects, however, this one shines the brightest: it was for her sister.

Knowing Gloria's taste, I stripped the colonial fireplace and created a very simple opening, a shelf; that was it. Then I removed the handrail spindles and replaced them with metal rods painted off-white. Upstairs, in an open balcony area, we placed all of her old furniture: the sectional sofa, round marble table, and leather chairs from Chicago, and added her old, Turkish Ouchak rug with a pale beige background. Her quality, classic furniture proved to be timeless.

On the first floor, our overall color scheme of white, gray, and black, helped the artwork stand out. For the dining room, Gloria purchased Italian-made furniture designed by Massimo and Lella Vignelli, two famous, Italian architects residing in New York. With elegance it sat on light, oak floors. A Roy Lichtenstein painting graced one wall, two Robert Motherwells, another.

The large living room opened up the downstairs. Under the staircase, I designed an off-white lacquer cabinet that could act as a buffet. It came all the way around into the living room where I had a black leather, three-piece sofa cut to fit into the corner. Over it, I hung an abstract painting by Joan Mitchell. Accented by a rug in white, black, and gray, the setting was striking.

A two-story fireplace was part of both the living and dining rooms. On the fireplace wall, I first placed a Frank Stella piece, but Gloria was not happy with that. I then found a wall hanging of light gray fabric that she preferred.

Adjacent to the dining room was a large kitchen with a center island. To complete it, I bought a streamlined table and chairs. Off the kitchen, we converted an area meant to be a breakfast nook into an office with a window. In addition, there was also a glassed-in porch off the living and dining areas which brought in the light.

The upper level had a small room that Gloria used for children's toys, a guest bedroom, two baths, a space with an office desk, and a bar. The entire home was eye-catching, perfect for entertaining, which Gloria loved to do. I was delighted to turn the traditional interior into a modern one. Gloria was thrilled, as well. When she had a party and I was there, she would say, "My sister did it all."

This project was uniquely wonderful. From my years of living with Gloria and traveling with her to Egypt and Japan, I knew her and her tastes. Like other projects, I presented the drawings and photographs of furniture for her approval. Unlike other residential projects, however, this one shines the brightest: it was for my sister.

"I WAS HAVING TROUBLE PUTTING TOGETHER THE COLOR SCHEME FOR THE PIERRE CARDIN EXHIBITION."

Chapter Four: Color

During the 1970s, I was a close friend and colleague of Hans Krieks, now deceased, a Holocaust survivor from Holland. When he was about sixteen, he was hidden by an apartment owner in a small attic. Because he had grown so tall, he had to hunch over while he stood. As it happened, Krieks took a liking to the owner's young daughter. To deter romance, the owner arranged to ship Krieks to another hideout. On the day after Krieks's evacuation, the Gestapo arrived at the apartment.

After World War II, Krieks came to the United States with his mother and started an interior design school where he taught furniture design and construction. In his office, he had a partner who knew a French gentleman in New York who represented Pierre Cardin. When Krieks heard that Cardin was interested in entering the United States market with his "Home Environment," we saw an opportunity to connect with Cardin. After lengthy deliberations, we signed a contract to become designers for Cardin's "Environment For the Home."

To prepare for the American premier exhibition, Krieks and I, with drawings in-hand, flew to Paris four times a year to show Cardin our work. We presented him with sketches and photographs of all our designs: case goods, upholstered pieces, rugs, fabrics, lighting—everything. With a nod or turn of his head, Cardin accepted or rejected our renderings. As we developed the line, Cardin sent me to Denmark to select the wool for carpets and to Italy to look at contemporary furniture. Krieks and I then worked with the licensees in America on the items that we wanted completed. Because Krieks was a skilled furniture designer, he could describe in detail to the factory personnel exactly how he wanted the pieces constructed for both appearance and comfort. Dillingham Manufacturing Company was selected to produce the furniture in North America, Ege Rya distributed floor coverings by Scandinavian Folklore Carpets of Denmark, and Laurel Lamps manufactured the lighting. It was a thrilling collection and collaboration.

I was responsible for creating the physical environment for the High Point, North Carolina, exhibition, where everything had to be coordinated in room settings. For me, the most difficult decision was determining a color scheme for the background of the Cardin furnishings, which had tones of beige, brown, silver, or gray. After learning about Dr. Jean Houston, an academic who offered a seminar on human potential, I decided to enroll.

At one of her sessions, she advised each participant to keep a piece of paper next to the bed and dream about a problem. Dutifully, before retiring one evening, I placed a pad of paper on my nightstand, closed my eyes, and thought about my color dilemma. At three o'clock in the morning, I awoke. Colors, which I never in the world would have thought of, appeared. Half-asleep, I scribbled down a color palette and went back to bed. That morning, at class, Dr. Houston inquired, "Did anybody have a dream?" When I raised my hand, she acknowledged me and I answered, "Yes, I found the color solution for the Pierre Cardin High Point showroom."

Cardin's "Environment For the Home" opened at four o'clock at the Southern Furniture Market on April 17, 1977, to great fanfare. Cardin, of course, came to High Point, North Carolina, and was very pleased. Interestingly, I remember that he admired my dress, a two-piece with pale blue stripes on a white background. Flattered, I thanked him and added, "I'm sorry that it is not your design." He replied that he was familiar with the fabric, which was from Italy, and that he had also used it. During those five years with Cardin, we were in constant contact. Work was invigorating. Moreover, during those years, I made more money in royalties than I ever made in my professional practice.

Each time I travel to Paris, I try to visit Boutique Pierre Cardin, 59 rue du Faubourg Saint-Honoré. I greet the lovely Maria, his former model, who is now the manager of the shop. Surprisingly, after over thirty years, she still remembers me. We embrace and reminisce about the times that I used to go upstairs where Cardin had his couturier clothes, that I was able to purchase at a tremendous discount. We recall a trip during the seventies when I watched her model a black-and-white

Above: Ruth and Hans Krieks with Pierre Cardin in his Paris office. Photo courtesy of "Archive Pierre Cardin."

print silk dress that I admired. I asked, "May I try it on?" "Of course," she responded. After I put it on, I said, "I'd love to have it." All they had to do was cut off about twelve inches. Otherwise, it fit perfectly. I then bought the dress and strolled out of the boutique, holding yet another one of the gorgeous pieces of Cardin clothing that I purchased during that time.

Several years ago, I met Cardin in New York for breakfast at the Plaza Athénée, a Manhattan hotel. With me, I brought the High Point portfolio and many of the press clippings. As he was paging through the album and looking at the photos, I asked, "Do you, by chance, have any of the furniture that I originally designed?" He answered, "Yes, in the house in Cannes. You are welcome to go down there." He, of course, was referring to the "Bubble House," his summer place in the South of France. That time, as always, Cardin was the most gracious of gentlemen.

Although I do not own any of the Cardin furniture that I designed, I have photographs of it. Several years ago, I went up near New Paltz, New York, to the home of Rolland Smith, a television commentator, humanitarian, and member of the International Center for Integrative Studies, (ICIS), for an ICIS salon. As I walked into the dining area, I noticed a Cardin buffet with double bands of chrome that I designed. Stunned, I inquired, "Where did you purchase this?" He said that he thought he bought it at Macy's. When I asked him discreetly about its price, he answered something like, "Six hundred dollars." Today it is worth ten thousand dollars; the value of each of Cardin's pieces has greatly appreciated. From time to time, I still see the Cardin furnishings for sale in *The New York Times* at a tremendous price.

My years of association with Pierre Cardin were extraordinary ones. He is an exemplary gentleman, whose mind and manner are ever-inspiring. Working for him, I experienced the meaning of "visionary." He and his designs prompt a peek at tomorrow.

My years of association with Pierre Cardin were extraordinary ones. He is an exemplary gentleman, whose mind and manner are ever-inspiring.

"TURNING INTERIOR DESIGN INTO A PROFESSION IS MY PASSION."

Chapter Five: Emphasis

Over forty years ago, I discovered my true passion: transforming interior design from an occupation into a profession. I attended a conference sponsored by the National American Society of Interior Designers, at which James Merrick Smith, then President, described his vision for creating a profession. He highlighted the importance of education, experience, and examination, the three facets necessary to achieve that transformation.

At the conference, Smith established several committees. I was fortunate to serve on two. One committee, the Foundation for Interior Design Education Research, had the responsibility of accreditation. Its members traveled around the United States and examined school programs in interior design to determine if they were qualified for certification. Today, that group is known as the Council for Interior Design Accreditation, or CIDA, and is recognized throughout the nation.

The second committee had the task of developing a comprehensive written examination; the chairman was Louis Tregre, from New York. Tregre, originally from New Orleans and now deceased, was an architect who specialized in interior design. I worked actively on that committee. As part of a pilot process, Tregre asked committee members to serve as guinea pigs and take the exam in our individual offices. After completion, we returned the exams to his office and were notified if we passed or failed. Tregre believed in our task. His fervor never faltered; he became my model. From criticism to acceptance, he never let go, remaining steadfast until his death in 1982. The National Council for Interior Design Qualifications, NCIDQ, oversees what has now become a two-day, three-part, written examination administered twice a year. It is accepted by every state.

Legislation, another aspect vital to Merrick's vision of a profession, had to be determined state by state. A few years after the conference, the New York City Chapter of the American Society of Interior Designers formed a group to decide whether it was time for New York State to go for legislation. A committee of approximately ten members voted to move ahead. They then needed someone to lead the campaign. No one volunteered. I realized that it was the proper time in my life to step forward.

> In 1984, I founded Interior Designers for Legislation in New York, and IDLNY, was born.

Jeffrey, Lance, Leslye, and Lloyd were grown, my design practice was thriving, and I had an able staff to take care of my work. I then asked myself, "Am I as willing, as Louis Tregre to stick with this responsibility as long as it takes to see if legislation can happen in New York State?" Feeling certain, I sought the approval of F.J. and our four children. After a favorable family vote, with one abstention from Lance, I accepted the challenge. In 1984, I founded Interior Designers for Legislation in New York, and IDLNY, was born.

At the time, New York had several interior design organizations, but it would not have been acceptable for each one individually to seek legislation. Therefore, I created a coalition of those organizations and brought the presidents, as well as educators, together for an initial meeting in Tregre's office on East 25th Street. We then continued to gather regularly to work on strategy. One of the members was Kerwin Kettler, a true scholar, and the Dean of the New York School of Interior Design.

He learned that in order for interior design to become a profession, we had to go through a series of state committees. The first one was Higher Education; Mark Alan Siegel served as its Chairman in the Assembly. Siegel informed us that in order to apply for licensure, we had to answer eighteen questions detailing how the interior design legislation supported the health, safety, and welfare of the public before he could proceed. Kettler then agreed to put together a response to the eighteen questions.

After reading our two-inch-thick, four-and-a-half-pound submission, Siegel decided to confer with us in Manhattan. I then organized a meeting at the office of Neville Lewis located near 26th Street. The reason I wanted us to go there was that Lewis had the largest interior design practice in New York City.

Previous page: Ruth in a moment of celebration after the bill was passed, holding a piece of Steuben crystal given to her by the students from all the interior design schools in New York State.

On the morning of our meeting with Siegel, we gathered in Lewis's conference room. Mark Alan Siegel sat at one end of a long, rectangular table; I sat at the other end. He looked at me and began, "Ruth Lynford, what are your qualifications?" So I told him that I had a degree in architecture and that I worked in interior design. He then went around the table, one-by-one, asking each individual about his/her qualifications. After that, Lewis and one of his assistants spoke about a large project in Colorado for which Lewis, an interior designer, was the first professional to be selected. It was then up to him to choose the architect to work on the endeavor. That was very impressive because normally the architect was selected first, then the interior designer.

After the presentation, we all walked to Lewis's drafting room where Siegel witnessed approximately one hundred twenty interior designers working on complex drawings. After the meeting, Siegel decided to allow the bill to go to the Higher Education Committee in the Assembly.

In my leadership role, I had to be concerned about money to support our enterprise, aware, of course, that New York is an expensive state to do anything. I realized the magnitude of the work ahead: I needed to have fund-raisers, hire a lobbyist, and acquire a public relations expert.

Through a suggestion from Fred Hersey, an interior designer from Albany, we hired a lobbyist, who then recommended Howard Rubenstein Associates, Inc., the most outstanding public relations firm in New York City, run, of course, by Howard J. Rubenstein. We interviewed him in Kettler's office on East 53rd Street. Rubenstein gave us a fee of ninety thousand dollars a year, which we agreed to pay. He then put in charge a woman, who specialized in New York State legislation.

One person who stood in our corner throughout the process was Beverly Russell, then editor-in-chief of the magazine *Interiors*. Believing in our cause, she arranged a luncheon at the University Club and invited presidents of several well-known furniture manufacturers. We planned the program carefully: Kettler spoke about the background and reason for the legislation, I talked about the proposed legislation, and Nina Hughes, an interior designer, discussed the need for fund-raising. During the gathering, three furniture manufacturers each committed a pledge of fifteen thousand dollars, giving us a forty-five-thousand-dollar nest egg. Russell, always held in high regard, then set into motion a series of luncheons similar to the first one.

When the American Institute of Architects (AIA), heard about our plans, there was immediate opposition. One opposing voice came from Lenore Lucey, from the New York Chapter of the AIA. She wrote a letter to *Interiors,* explaining their objections. Russell published it. The following month, she published a letter written by me in response to Lucey's position. That back-and-forth went on for approximately a year.

I then started frequent trips to Albany where I met Jim Yates, the counsel to Mel Miller, Speaker of the House. He understood IDLNY's goals and rationale and supported our cause, even though his wife was an architect. After several unsuccessful years, however, we determined that the lobbying firm we had hired was not for us; we wanted one that allowed us to participate in the process. With the help of Rubenstein, we then hired Davidoff & Malito, LLP, a firm that had offices in Manhattan and Albany. That firm assigned Jack Bronston, a lawyer and former New York State senator, to be in charge of our account. He was terrific. Bronston studied the issues, met with me frequently, and took me along with him to lobby the legislators.

> At a little before midnight on July 1, 1990, our bill, number A.10409-A, passed unanimously in the Assembly.

All the while, Rubenstein served as a valuable supporter. He introduced our team to a woman who taught us how to speak quickly, succinctly, and clearly, since we often had only a minute to talk with a legislator. For follow-up communication, we were coached on letter writing skills, which further aided our direction.

Toward the end of one of the sessions, a moment of particular import occurred. I wanted to see Saul Weprin, the Chairman of the Ways and Means Committee in the assembly, before the bill went to the floor of the legislature. For three days, I sat waiting in front of his office hoping to see him. In frustration, I made a telephone call one Friday afternoon to Rubenstein, who was on his way to Pound Ridge, where he had a weekend house. I said, "Howard, I've tried for three days to see Saul Weprin. Is there anything that you can do for me?" He responded, "Yes, you should go back." When I returned to the waiting area, the receptionist said, "Saul Weprin will see you now." And, in I walked. So, Howard Rubenstein certainly opened doors.

Over the years in Albany, even amid the ongoing objections from the American Institute of Architects, Yates remained constant. Two additional steady forces were Oliver Koppell, a gifted orator who became our sponsor in the Assembly, and Kenneth LaValle, who served as our sponsor in the Senate. When Koppell asked Michael Garabedian, his key staff person, to sit down with me and work out the legislative points, I continued to negotiate with the two architects from the AIA, but I did not get very far.

Finally, during the last few days of the legislative session, Yates received the approval to tell the AIA, that unless they negotiated with the Interior Designers for Legislation in New York, the legislators were going to write the law. Of course, the AIA did not want that to occur. Three days before the end of the legislative session, I met with the two architects. To help craft the exact wording, I telephoned Martin Zelnick and several other architects and designers.

In seventy-two hours, we knocked out the verbiage of the bill. There were, of course, to be specifications which Koppell had discussed with Kettler and me three weeks prior to the legislation. We had to give up grandfathering and agree that all applicants seeking licensure had to successfully complete the National Council for Interior Design Qualifications Examination (NCIDQ).

On the last night of the New York State Legislative session, when each house voted on the agenda of the various bills, I was present. The only person with me was Garabedian from Koppell's office. Although he and I could not be seated on the floor, we sat in the balcony where we could see and hear what was going on. Suspended overhead, Garabedian and I listened expectantly as Koppell spoke on our behalf. He was absolutely eloquent. At a little before midnight on July 1, 1990, our bill, number A.10409-A, passed unanimously in the Assembly.

Immediately, Garabedian and I decided that we had to rush over to the Senate side. Even though Bronston was not in Albany that evening, we knew that his firm was friendly with the head of the Senate. The Senate, however, needed to have something in writing from the Assembly to verify that the bill had passed. Because the Assembly had already adjourned, we scrambled around trying to find either Koppell or Ed Sullivan, the Higher Education Chairman in the Assembly. Luckily, we located Sullivan, who, by hand, verified that the bill had passed.

At a little past midnight, the Senate was still in session. The bills to be voted on appeared on an agenda. Calendar after calendar was presented. At close to seven o'clock in the morning, our bill had not yet been on one of them. In desperation, and in those wee hours, I called Bronston. He, in turn, called his boss, who then phoned the head of the Senate. Our bill, number S.7609-A, was the last one listed on the final calendar.

Seated in the Albany balcony with Garabedian, I heard LaValle, our Senate sponsor, speak earnestly on our behalf. The gavel went down. At seven o'clock Monday morning, July 2, 1990, we had a law. We had witnessed a miracle.

I had no one from Interior Designers for Legislation in New York, IDLNY, with me, so I dashed to an outdoor telephone booth. The first person I called was Kettler, my anchor, and exclaimed, "Kerwin, we have a law!" Without Kettler, New York would not have had one.

I then boarded Amtrak and rode to Manhattan alone. In "seventh heaven," I did not notice the whirr of the rails or my lack of sleep. Euphoric, I took a taxi from Pennsylvania Station to my apartment, picked up the telephone receiver, and continued making calls. I told everyone, "We gave birth." Tears filled my eyes knowing what we had all been through.

> Shortly after our bill was passed, I went to Howard Rubenstein's office to hang photographs of some of his clients. He said, "Ruth, I never thought you could do it." I responded, "Howard, I'm so glad you told me this now, and not before the bill was passed."

It took IDLNY about six years to accomplish legislation at a cost of five million dollars. Some interior designers were unhappy because they had to take and pass the exam; others were angry because we had to give up the grandfather clause. The legislation, however, was voluntary, not mandatory. Most importantly, we had secured a Voluntary Title Act creating the title of "Certified Interior Designer." On July 30, 1990, when Governor Mario M. Cuomo inscribed his signature, interior design became the thirty-third profession in the bellwether State of New York.

I knew that when the bill became a law, it was time for me to step down as president of Interior Designers for Legislation in New York. I selected Carolyn Brooks, an extremely bright woman, to assume the presidency. I had met her when she was with ISD, an interior design firm that I took legislators to visit. She and her colleague Linda

96 | My Life in Design

Jacobs had brilliantly educated the lawmakers on the differences between interior designers and interior decorators. With their detailed explanations and drawings, the two of them showed how interior designers are problem solvers, licensed to understand building codes, and who can design lighting and dropped ceilings, and move only non-bearing walls.

Early on as president, Carolyn Brooks cleverly got the balance of our ninety thousand dollar lobbying fee reduced to half, allowing IDLNY finally to take care of that obligation. With her presidency, she took up the gauntlet and led with grace.

Shortly after our bill was passed, I went to Howard Rubenstein's office to hang photographs of some of his clients. He said, "Ruth, I never thought you could do it." I responded, "Howard, I'm so glad you told me this now, and not before the bill was passed."

As I look back, I realize that IDLNY nudged me to heed my past. As a child, I was taught to take risks and put my life on the line for what I felt was right. With zeal, many years later, I sprang into action and we achieved our goal.

"TO CONTINUE THE MOMENTUM, I ONCE AGAIN STEPPED TOWARDS EDUCATION."

2013 Interior Design Student Exhibition

New York Eleven Plus

INTERIOR DESIGN: A NEW YORK PERSPECTIVE

Chapter Six: Rhythm

In the mid 1990s, a single invitation proved to be life-changing. I was invited to a conference at the United Nations coordinated by Professor Diane Davis, founder of the International Council for Caring Communities. Delegates from all over the world attended. A portion of the program featured a competition among students from various architectural schools to design a facility for an aging population. While sitting next to an architect who taught interior design at Pratt Institute, I asked, "Why aren't the interior designer design students who do interiors for the aging represented here?" He said, "Why don't you discuss that with Diane Davis? She is the one who put this all together." At the end of the conference, I went to see her and asked her why the interior design profession was not represented. She told me that if I wanted it included, I might see what I could create.

My idea was to gather together the department chairs of the six accredited interior designs schools in the metropolitan area: the New York School of Interior Design, the New York Institute of Technology, Parsons The New School, the Fashion Institute of Technology, Pratt Institute, and the School of Visual Arts. I then arranged a breakfast meeting for us at one of the United Nations buildings. The chairs remembered me through the licensing legislation and all six attended. When I informed them about the conference and the student-architect competition and inquired if they would be interested in participating, they said, "Yes," but they did not want a competition. They preferred an exhibition. Planning began. I requested that each school select a project on the aging, prepare drawings, and choose someone to speak about it. They all responded.

The annual date for the United Nations Conference had been set; again, the topic was aging. Haworth Incorporated delivered fabric panels to a large exhibition space for us to present the work of the senior students from the six schools. In preparation, I met, two weeks in advance, with each student representative, so that the five-minute presentation would be articulate, clear, and engaging.

Above: Ruth and David Bright, Manager Knoll Showroom, New York, in the Knoll Showroom

Previous page: Cover of the New York Eleven Plus invitation to the 2013 Student Exhibition

After the opening general session, delegates from countries across the globe were able to listen to the students' ideas and take them back to replicate in their homelands. Hearing the students and seeing their visions, the delegates became aware of not only the complexities, but also the rigor of interior design education. Open for one week, the exhibition was a huge success. Because the student projects were so impressive the first year, we were asked to come back the following year for two weeks and given additional space.

The third year, the United Nations invited us to have our exhibition in the main lobby for one month. At the time, John Lijewski, a mentee of mine when he had been a student at Parsons and one of my "designing children," served as President of the New York Chapter of the International Interior Design Association, IIDA. He, as president of the organization, generously arranged to give me a twenty thousand dollar donation, so that we could set up a professional display, which he supervised. That year, Nane Annan, wife of then Secretary General of the United Nations Kofi A. Annan, attended the opening. She viewed the exhibit, spoke about it, and helped us cut the ribbon. Afterwards, we held a celebratory reception.

At the end of that exhibition, the six schools decided to include the upstate schools in the following year. Cornell University, Syracuse University, Buffalo State, Cazenovia College, and Rochester Institute of Technology expressed interest, but did not want to come to Manhattan. We then agreed to hold the exhibition in Albany at the Legislative Office Building, adjacent to the capitol.

In 1997, eleven schools skillfully displayed their talents. The schools represented were prestigious New York State colleges and universities, all having four-year- or- more programs in interior design. On the opening night, the Higher Education Chairmen of both the Assembly and Senate, and Ronald Canestrari, the Majority Leader of the

Assembly, participated. At the ribbon-cutting ceremony, they each spoke briefly about the event, and were given scissors. I counted "One, two, three." In unison, we snipped the ribbon and New York Eleven was born. In collaboration, students and educators stimulated awareness of the power of design among the legislators, press, design professionals, and public.

Each spring either in March or April, the New York Eleven, now Eleven Plus, displays the student work. As stated on its publicity, its enduring mission is: "to emphasize the complexity and responsibility of the interior design profession, particularly as it pertains to the health, safety, welfare, and economics of the public."

On the first day of the exhibition, we invite design students, in addition to the ones selected to hang their work, to join in a Student Lobby Day. Cassandra Ramirez, the New York Eleven Plus Coordinator, often arranges to have a bus in front of the Fashion Institute of Technology on 27th and 7th Avenues to take the young designers to Albany. Some students hang their work in booth-created areas; other students attend orientation sessions given by Jan Dorman, the Executive Director of IDLNY. He tells them about the issues of pertinent legislation, what they should talk about, and divides them into teams according to their school's legislative district. For about two to three hours, the students lobby and then return in time for the five-thirty, ribbon-cutting ceremony and reception. After that, they board the bus for the trip back to Manhattan. The day is rich with energy and information.

We then arrange for a trucking company to pack all the work displayed and bring it to Manhattan to a hosting showroom such as Teknion, Haworth, or Knoll. The local students again hang their work. Cassandra Ramirez, the coordinator, sets up the submissions of the upstate schools according to their instructions. Because Manhattan has less space than Albany, we give each individual school approximately fifteen linear feet. Following the Manhattan ribbon-cutting ceremony and reception, we hold a half-hour program featuring a topic with a related speaker, panel, and/or media presentation for the students and professionals attending. Afterwards, we treat several patrons and sponsors to dinner at the Metropolitan Club.

After the Manhattan exhibition is completed, we have what is called a "Post Mortem Meeting," and invite the chairs from all the schools. They discuss what they liked and disliked about the Albany and Manhattan events. We then determine a focus and a title for he following year. For two years we chose "Interior Design: Sustaining the Future, 1 and 2." Another year, we selected "Enriching the Community." Jamie Drake spoke on residential interior design and Shashi Caan, on commercial design. One year, our theme was, "Protecting the Public" and Tama Duffy Day, an

Rhythm | 103

Above: Ruth and Majority Leader, Ronald Canestrari. Ruth's movement from Interior Designers for Legislation in New York to the New York Eleven Plus was a natural one. The two organizations intersect. The legislators have to be educated and the students need to understand the legislative process.

international interior designer from Washington, D.C., with Perkins+Will, explored her specialty, therapeutic environments. In 2013 the title of the exhibition will be "Interior Design: A New York Perspective."

Each year as New York Eleven Plus evolves, the student work becomes increasingly complex and stimulating. Through participation, the students learn the scope and depth of interior design, see what other schools are teaching, and meet and speak with other students, interior design professionals, and state legislators. In collaboration, we inform, inspire, and build the interior design profession. As defined in its mission, "New York Eleven seeks to advance the purpose of interior design by demonstrating solutions to cultural problems, such as the diminution of natural resources, aging population, ecological issues, and other social concerns." With its recent classification as a not-for-profit 501(c)(3) organization, New York Eleven Plus can be supported more ably by industry and others to further develop its work. Since its inception, New York Eleven Plus has grown into a community of professionals that is happy, healthy, and humane.

My movement from Interior Designers for Legislation in New York to the New York Eleven Plus was a natural one. The two organizations intersect. The legislators have to be educated and the students need to understand the legislative process. The two fit together well, forming a perfect interaction of two entities involved in interior design. In tandem, their rhythm informs our daily lives, helping us to live safely and wholly in our interiors.

"STEADYING
MY PACE, I
MOVED FORWARD
WITH ICIS."

Chapter Seven: Harmony

My daily walk on the planet expanded in the mid-1970s. Attending an event at the United Nations, I met Dr. Janis A. Roze, a herpetologist, a professor of biology, and one of the founders of the International Center for Integrative Studies (ICIS), a non-governmental organization (NGO) of the United Nations. He invited me to visit their facilities located on the corner of 18th Street and 6th Avenue. I accepted. One evening, I accompanied him to The Door, an ICIS project occupying a gigantic, approximately sixty-thousand-square-foot interior.

The Door, A Center of Alternatives, was created to help inner-city youth, ages thirteen to twenty, with their life challenges. It was and still is a model for organizations around the globe; visitors from Australia came to see it so that they could replicate the concept. The lower level had medical rooms, legal offices, and psychological services. The first floor had a gymnasium, a theatre, and all kinds of recreational activities for young people in the neighborhood. On the balcony, ICIS had its office.

ICIS was formed in 1962, by Erling A. Thunberg, a visionary from Sweden who came to the United States as a young man, believing in an interdisciplinary model for living and learning. He saw it as a way for all disciplines to interact, a way toward human potential. Erling Thunberg, Janis Roze, Lamar Carter, George A. Christie, Donald F. Keys, and E. Alice Beard all participated in transforming this idea into action. As they discussed ideas, they attempted to implement them. That was how The Door was brought into being.

In addition, ICIS established *The Forum,* a bound, printed document published four times a year, which included excerpts of ideas from scholars throughout the world. It was distributed with the hope that others might respond to the articles and generate an interdisciplinary and intracultural dialogue. In 1962, ICIS became a not-for-profit 501(c)(3) organization.

In December 2012, ICIS celebrated its fifty-year anniversary. Its rich history and mission are highlighted in a July 20, 2012 invitation letter which states: "ICIS is a fully engaged, non-governmental organization (NGO), accredited with the United Nations whose mission is to advance interdisciplinary communication and cooperation among the humanities, behavioral, social, and life sciences. From its inception in 1962, the goal of ICIS has been to bring together diverse perspectives to co-create a common vision for the positive future of humanity. Through its programs and activities, ICIS works to identify, synthesize, and disseminate leading edge thinking, with the purpose of demonstrating new ways of approaching societal and world concerns."

Because of Dr. Roze, I became very interested in ICIS and The Door. Originally, ICIS had a building lease which started at about four dollars a square foot. Ten years later, the neighborhood began gentrifying and the landlord raised the fee to ten dollars a square foot. Over time, the rent had increased to the point that ICIS could not afford it and had to look for other options.

As an active member of ICIS and involved with several design schools, I volunteered to take an ICIS project idea to The Fashion Institute of Design: the students would design two facilities for ICIS, one in the existing building, the other in a different building. Excited, I went to see Martin Zelnick, the architect who chaired the Interior Design Department at the Fashion Institute of Technology and an ardent advocate of real-life challenges for students. He turned the project over to Michael Altschuler, another architect instructor, who then divided one class into two teams. Six weeks later, the teams had completed the floor plans, elevations, and models.

I then asked the ICIS board members to come to The Fashion Institute of Technology to see the student presentation. They were very impressed and decided to take all the drawings, the models, and everything that the students produced to the Ford Foundation. After seeing the student efforts, the Ford Foundation agreed to give ICIS a four million dollar donation over a period of four years, all because of the exceptional student work and the superior accomplishments of The Door.

> "...the goal of ICIS has been to bring together diverse perspectives to co-create a common vision for the positive future of humanity. Through its programs and activities, ICIS works to identify, synthesize, and disseminate leading edge thinking, with the purpose of demonstrating new ways of approaching societal and world concerns."
>
> July 20, 2012
> ICIS Letter

Previous page: Ruth with Ambassador Hardeep Singh Puri, who is the Permanent Representative of India to the United Nations. Ambassador Puri spoke at the ICIS Salon, September 21, 2012.

The ICIS Board then decided to purchase a building down on Spring Street that they converted into offices; only non-profit groups could occupy the space. Michael Altschuler, the instructor at The Fashion Institute of Technology, was hired as the architect. He designed three floors for The Door: the basement and the upper two floors. The top floor was sold to the Fund of the City of New York.

In keeping with a community spirit, some of the ICIS founders and staff purchased loft space in an apartment building on 13th Street where they lived, and originally had ICIS salons. Near the entrance of the apartments was a large room with semicircular, auditorium-style seating. Each corner of the room held antique items that Thunberg had acquired from his travels to many different cultures.

In time, The Door and ICIS separated; The Door became one entity, ICIS, another. The Door, however, was and still is an innovative phenomenon. It demonstrates the ICIS spirit, an interdisciplinary approach to problem solving with an emphasis on humanity. For a while, ICIS continued having office space in the same building on 6th Avenue, but because of lack of funds, it could no longer afford to remain there. The Door is currently located at 555 Broome Street between Varick Street and 6th Avenue. Most of the ICIS work is presently conducted at founder Lamar Carter's apartment in Greenwich Village.

In 2002, ICIS reintroduced the salon, which takes place in my Manhattan apartment. Every month, we invite about two hundred guests, even though I am able to seat only fifty in my living room. The first forty-five individuals who respond are accepted. Although certain people attend regularly, once in a while others join in: friends of the board, friends of friends, and guests. A few have been known to leave town or move out of the country and come back a year or two later. It is a very fluid and popular event.

Sarajane Brittis, Ph.D., current President of ICIS, and Bruce Cohen, Esq., a board member, serve as the ICIS representatives to the United Nations. They attend the weekly lectures and recommend possible speakers to the Salon Committee. We then invite potential speakers to have lunch at the Metropolitan Club; if they are interested in participating, we set a date.

During the past ten years, we have held more than sixty salons on an array of topics. One time Hans-Peter Dürr, Ph.D., a quantum physicist who is a member of the Board of Directors of the Max-Planck Institute for Physics and Astrophysics in Germany, held a "Conversation on Science and Consciousness." At another salon, Joshua Cooper Ramo, Managing Director of Kissinger Associates, spoke about his 2009 book,

Harmony | 111

> Each month, I sit, at rest, on a tiny Louis XVI oval footstool that I had antiqued white to blend in with the living room chairs. No one in the salon has yet been able to fit on that stool.

The Age of the Unthinkable: Why the New World Disorder Constantly Surprises Us and What We Can Do About It. Dr. Debbie Joffe Ellis, whose husband Albert Ellis was a famous psychologist, talked about, "Coping Well With Adversities: the Remarkable Life of Albert Ellis and the Application of His Wisdom to Our Own Lives." So, we have had a variety of stimulating subjects and speakers, and with each salon our conversations continue and we are enriched.

Recently, I have been called a " Saloniere," perhaps, because I am Jewish and hold monthly meetings in my apartment living room. Although I am certainly not as recognized or affluent as Gertrude Stein or Fanny Mendelssohn, I am inspired. Each month, I sit, at rest, on a tiny Louis XVI oval footstool that I had antiqued white to blend in with the living room chairs. It is upholstered with a French needlepoint fabric, detailed with maroon morning glories.

No one in the salon has yet been able to fit on that stool. No one is that little. As if by habit, I take my place. Perched peacefully on those four legs, I listen.

"LIFE, LIKE DESIGN, DEMANDS A DELICATE BALANCE; IT IS AGILITY THAT GIVES ME PLEASURE."

Chapter Eight: Balance

Every place holds possibilities and I discovered just that, in Venice. About a year and a half after F.J. died, I went to Italy on a conference trip for architects and interior designers. When I arrived in Milan, I was introduced to Lillian Weinreich, an architect who grew up in Australia. She asked me to room with her; I agreed and we spent the remainder of the trip together.

Six hundred and thirty-four architects and designers assembled from all over the world and stayed in five hotels. During the day, groups were assigned different responsibilities. At night, we all gathered together in a large auditorium to listen to speeches, often given by Italian architects who never had the intention or ability to find a job in the profession. Many of them designed furniture or items for the office or home. Apparently, they thought that architecture provided a good background for any endeavor.

Every evening after the speakers, Lillian and I met in our room and discussed the happenings of the day. One night, after we had an afternoon of personal shopping, she mentioned, "Ruth, I met the nicest gentleman, Arthur Steinberg, an architect from Texas. He is too old for me, but maybe he would be great for you." As a widow for a short time, I really was not interested in meeting anyone, but I listened to her, and we continued talking.

During the trip, I had already been introduced to Gary, an American architect, practicing in Hawaii. One evening as some of us were about to have dinner at a restaurant, a group of American students helped us read the Italian menu. I then went over to another table, where Arthur Steinberg and three others waited to dine, and said, "If you need any help with translation, the American students will happily assist. After eating, our group boarded a bus. I sat next to a window and Gary was seated next to me. Across the aisle from Gary sat Arthur Steinberg, who began talking across Gary to me.

Our conference groups then divided for travel to different cities, and returned to Venice for an Architectural Biennale. In order to get to the exhibition, we had to take a boat from one island to another. As it happened, Arthur Steinberg sat next to me

Balance | 117

on the boat. In our brief conversation, he told me that he was a widower of two-and-a-half years; I told him that I was a widow.

A couple of days later, on a rainy afternoon in Venice, I found free time to shop. Without an umbrella and with hair dripping down, I turned into a little via. Arthur turned into the same via from an opposite direction. When we saw each other, he walked over, embraced me, and asked, "Do you have a card?" I gave him my business card. He then told me that he was leaving the following day to go back to Texas. I mentioned that I was heading to Rome to visit Brigitta Goeritz, my fine, former design assistant.

Three days later, at home in Manhattan, I received a telephone call from Arthur who said, "I'm coming to New York on business. Could we have lunch?" I responded, "Of course," and suggested the Metropolitan Club, across the street from my apartment, where I am a member.

Dressed in a jacket and tie, Arthur stood waiting in the lobby. At first, I did not recognize him because on the trip, no one dressed up and he was relaxed and casual. At lunch, we talked for three hours. During our chatter, I somehow mentioned that my maiden name was Kahn. He then asked, "Are you Jewish?" I said, "Yes." He was delighted. That was the beginning of the romance.

In the subsequent months, he invited me to go to New Orleans, where he graduated from Tulane University in architecture, and to Houston, where he lived. In Texas, I stayed in a hotel, because his late wife's mother still lived in the beautiful house that he designed, and he was embarrassed to have me be there. But after several visits, he felt comfortable enough for me to stay. We became very close. One day, he said, "Ruth, I think I'd be interested in getting married in about two years." Well, I was six years older, and not about to wait that long. I told him, "Arthur, I'm not the right woman for you."

Opposite page, Top: Ruth and Arthur's engagement photo taken at Steelcase. Bottom: Wedding photo of Ruth and Arthur with their families

Balance | 119

Prior to my visits, Arthur had been seeing a psychologist who was helping him work out of the depression following his wife's death. On an earlier visit, he introduced me to her. When I returned to New York, Arthur told her about our conversation. She said, "If you're really in love with this lady and you want to marry her, you better decide right now or you're going to lose her."

A few weeks later when I returned to Houston, Arthur took me to Tony's, a noted restaurant, and on an August evening presented me with a card on which he proposed marriage. Arthur then came to New York, where we visited Leslye, my daughter, and announced our engagement and the date of our May wedding. We wanted to get married in warm weather, so that we could have an outdoor ceremony. I then looked at Rachel, Lesyle's daughter, and asked, "Rachel, would you like to be a flower girl?" She answered, "Of course, Grandma." I turned to Julia, Lloyd's younger daughter, and she said, "Oh, yes." And then I walked over to Sophie, Lloyd's older daughter, who at that time was ten and preferred slacks to dresses and asked, "Sophie, if you are willing to wear a dress, would you be a flower girl?" She replied, "Grandma, I'll think about it." An hour later, Sophie announced, "Grandma, I'm willing to wear a dress." We had three flower girls, all granddaughters, for our wedding day. My other grandchildren, Victoria, Drew, Alex, Ben, Hugh, and Kirsten and Dylan, my daughter-in-law Tondra's two daughters, were also to be important guests at our wedding.

When I went back to Houston, we told Arthur's children, Tami, Marci, and Sanford, also an architect, who then planned an engagement party in Tami's home in Sugarland, designed by Sanford. The February festivity was complete with music, mirth, and food. A few guests asked, "Why are you getting married and not just living together?" Arthur spoke, "I love this woman, I want to spend the rest of my life with her, and I believe in marriage." Of course, after that, all the couples looked at one another, applauded, and resumed the celebration.

With Arthur came a fine family—Tami, Marci, Sanford, two granddaughters, Sharon and Melanie, and, more recently, two great-grandsons, Jacob and Ryan. At twenty-one, I found what I wanted in F.J.—an outgoing, energetic, entrepreneur. Arthur was different, a very quiet, poet type. I enjoyed both. Never would I have been smitten at age twenty-one, the way I was at seventy-two with Arthur.

When Arthur and I decided to marry after our chance meeting, our romance produced yet another project, a residential one. I owned a one-bedroom, one-bath, Manhattan apartment at 785 Fifth Avenue that F.J. and I purchased when he was alive. It was, however, too tiny for Arthur and me to live in full-time, even with Arthur's large home in Texas. As it happened, the unit directly below mine went up for sale. Arthur decided to buy it. We were then going to break through and make a duplex when we married, so that we would have two bedrooms and two bathrooms. In preparation, we received clearance from the building to combine the apartments.

Three months before our wedding, there was a knock on my door. Phyllis Engler, a building resident, told me that she had heard that we were getting married and wondered if we might be interested in buying her apartment and if I might be willing to sell mine. She owned an apartment on the sixth floor, overlooking Central Park, and was about to downsize, but hoped to stay in the building. When Arthur and I looked at her two-bedroom, two-bath apartment, we thought that it might be a smart idea to live on one floor as we grew older, instead of quibbling about who was going to use which bathroom. We then agreed to purchase it, and gave Phyllis a choice: Arthur's unit on the sixth floor or mine on the seventh. Years earlier, with the help of Steve Louie and Tse Yun Chu, I had totally gutted and redesigned the entire interior of my unit, which made it move-in ready. Phyllis chose mine.

Arthur then decided to sell his apartment. I mentioned that to my son Jeffrey whose business was in Manhattan, but whose home was in Katonah, New York. He, like his father and mother, wanted a pied-à-terre. After talking with Tondra, his wife, he decided to purchase Arthur's. So we played musical apartments. Arthur and I bought 6A. I sold 7D to Phyllis, and Jeffrey bought 6D from Arthur. We needed no agents or brokers.

On May 25, 1998, Arthur Steinberg and I were married at King House in Tarrytown, New York. The ceremony took place around noon and was followed by a brief reception and lunch. Lloyd, my youngest, an eloquent speaker known for his

Balance | 121

wit, spoke for about ten minutes. During his toast, we cried and laughed, but the words that stuck were: "When the four Lynford children met Arthur, they didn't know how this relationship was going to work, because Arthur is so laid-back and my mother is like a tank commander at El Alamein." After the luncheon, Arthur and I came back to Manhattan and stayed at the Sherry Netherland, next door to our apartment. The following morning, we began our glorious, two-week, Italian honeymoon to Venice, Tuscany, and Lake Como, complete with pasta and Chianti.

Upon our return, we settled into Arthur's apartment at 6D, until our new one, 6A, was ready. We decided to bring in Jim Vaughn, a young designer friend of mine, to help us with the 6A renovation. Although we did not gut it, we did extensive work, which included the ceilings and lighting. A nice thing about Arthur and me was that we worked well together; our egos were harmonious.

When the construction was completed, I took all the furniture that was not built-in, from 7D to 6A and then added only a few items. I believe in versatility, using and reusing well-designed, well-made furniture, over and over, and not sparingly. A simple chest should be able to be used in a bedroom, an entrance foyer, a dining room, or a living room.

I moved the French antique armoire with a bonnet that F.J. bought on 3rd Avenue and converted it into a bar. It fit nicely into the niche in the living room. The sixty-inch, round, drop-leaf, English table that we sat around at Sunday dinner in West Nyack was placed near our front window. Two Louis XVI antique chairs that we used when dining sit nearby. In the bedroom, I set up the table and four chairs from West Nyack, for use at breakfast. Best of all, the furniture connected the past to the present, thus creating a feeling of home.

Opposite page: So they played musical apartments. Arthur and Ruth bought 6A. Ruth sold 7D to Phyllis, and Jeffrey bought 6D from Arthur. They needed no agents or brokers.

Arthur and I moved into the apartment and happily enjoyed our days. Arthur sold the large house he designed in Houston and bought a lovely apartment in the Galleria area. We then traveled to Thailand, Hong Kong, and Bali and lived joyfully until his untimely death in 2002, only four years later.

Since 1979, after moving from West Nyack, I have resided in Parc V, where I plan to stay forever. From the windows, I gaze out above the treetops over Central Park and take in each day, week, month, and season. The skyscape and landscape renew me. In the nearly sixteen-hundred-square-foot interior, I find the equilibrium necessary for adventure.

My days are filled with professional activity, which began years ago as a student at Washington University in St. Louis, when I was a student member of the American Society of Interior Designers (ASID). It continued, years later, in New York as the Chairman of the Student Council, where I met "The Three Musketeers"—Steve Louie from Pratt, Bryan English also from Pratt, and John Lijewski from Parsons. They were all buddies; the Student Council united the trio and kept them together. In 1974, we traveled to the national conference in Denver, Colorado. Wearing a simple white pleated full-length dress, I attended a black-tie event. There I was surprised with the news that I was the recipient of the Fellowship Award. After the dinner, the students said, "We're going up to the roof to go swimming." Caught in their spirit, I went up there with them, took off my diamond watch, gave it to Bryan, and jumped in with my nylon dress clinging to me. It was baptism into the fellowship, and that was quite an honor. Many years later, the three of them are established, outstanding professionals, who remain in contact with me and will forever be "my designing children."

I also continue my close alliance with Washington University in St. Louis in several ways, specifically as a

> Since 1979, after moving from West Nyack, I have resided in Parc V, where I plan to stay forever. From the windows, I gaze out above the treetops over Central Park and take in each day, week, month, and season. The skyscape and landscape renew me. In the nearly sixteen-hundred-square-foot interior, I find the equilibrium necessary for adventure.

long-time member of the National Council of the Sam Fox School of Design & Visual Arts and, more recently in 2010, as a distinguished alumnus. In 2005, I received a Distinguished Alumni Award from the School of Architecture. That particular recognition carried both joy and sadness.

For consideration, I was asked to submit a portfolio showing all past work, which in my case, included over fifty years of documentation. Foolishly, on my part I included originals of everything—wonderful, large photographs of my commercial and residential projects. For the occasion, they were on display, as was everyone else's work. At the event, each of the honorees received a gift, an exquisite light green crystal bowl.

After the ceremony, I asked that someone from Washington University ship it to me, so that I would not have to transport it on the plane. A week later, the box arrived well-packed with bubble wrap. I removed the bowl from the carton, looked at the bottom, saw nothing and threw it away. Three days later, I called an assistant at the university and asked if someone would please return my portfolio. I was then told that it had been placed at the bottom of the shipping box. Out went fifty years of photographs; there was nothing to be done. Although I do have a few duplicates, I have nothing to compare to the portfolio. That work is now charted in my soul. Happily, my allegiance to Washington University remains, and proves to be steady.

Since I became a design fellow and the founder of Interior Designers for Legislation in New York and New York Eleven Plus, I continue to strive with professionals at all levels to raise the bar of interior design. This is my passion. Together with other interior designers, we ask the important, ever-changing questions to those in all disciplines in search of solutions for a more humane, sustainable, world environment for every individual. This work, although often messy, gives meaning to my days.

My immediate and lifetime goal is to upgrade the status of the interior design profession and get a "Practice Act" by the time I am ninety. I am determined that this should happen. Several years ago, when I visited the Society of Interior Designers National Headquarters in Washington, D.C., I met with Don Davis, the gentleman in charge of Government Relations. He asked, "Ruth, have you ever thought of amending the law that you got passed in 1990, to have a Practice Act?" Well, he put a bee in my bonnet. I hope to be able to introduce a bill in January, 2013, creating a "Practice Act" for interior designers in New York State.

The bill will allow licensed interior designers to stamp and seal their drawings in order to be accepted by the Building Department and will also allow them to become members of professional corporations presently reserved to four disciplines: architects, engineers, landscape surveyors, and urban-planners. I am optimistic that if the bill passes, it will encourage designers to become licensed, so that they, too, can then become partners in the firms in which they work. We want to place interior designers in a position to become partners, if they are asked. This recognition would bring about an improvement in their livelihoods. Hand-in-hand, we must educate interior designers, students, and the public about the importance of accomplishing this goal.

So, I have much work and many headaches to look forward to. My frequent trips to Albany will continue into the future. I am known there. The legislators say, "There she is!" It will be expensive. We will have to do fund-raising, hire a lobbyist, select a sponsor in both the Assembly and the Senate, and do the same things we did before. And we will still have opposition. It is a big undertaking, but we are on the mark, and I am set and ready to go for the challenge.

At heart, part of me is still the "little boat" anchored on Bamberger Avenue in St. Louis, near the Mississippi. Another part is securely docked on Fifth Avenue in Manhattan. Now at work in a part-time interior design practice, I experience a newly balanced life. Near and with my treasured family, I listen to Rachmaninoff, attend the Metropolitan Opera, visit the Neue Galerie, dine at the Metropolitan Club, enjoy the theatre, travel to Paris, meet with friends, dance the tango, and work out with a trainer. With humanity, I continue rowing, hitting high waters, raising the bar, and finding my place—all part of a dream, designed.

IN WORD
AND DEED,
RUTH IS
DYNAMIC.

Chapter Nine: Texture and Shape

The following reflections are from a few associates who know Ruth in action. They elaborate on the warp and woof of Ruth's life in design. Adding specific dimensions, they comment on the work and play of her head, heart, and hands. As they touch upon the light and dark, smoothness and roughness, their words give shape and life.

Sanna Feirstein, Former Partner

The first words that come to mind when I think of Ruth are: generous, elegant, and tenacious. Others are: warm, intelligent, creative, energetic, thoughtful, and inclusive. I could go on. As I discovered when I first worked for Ruth, she is an unusually generous teacher, sharing her encyclopedic knowledge of the design field with no restrictions. No one works harder and with more dedication to a project than Ruth. She is a warm and thoughtful friend to a host of lucky individuals. Together, we've watched each other's families evolve over many years.

Perhaps my fondest memories of our work life together involve moments when we simply collapsed in laughter. We were a bit of Mutt and Jeff with Ruth as the diminutive powerhouse and me as the (relatively) Amazonian amanuensis. This contrast provided comic moments as when, at the end of a meeting aimed at securing a client, we both tried to fit through the same narrow doorway at the same time. But there were more of the day-to-day moments which simply tickled us and ended in gales of giggles.

Ruth helped me through rough times, and I like to think that I helped her through some of her own. Most importantly, from her I learned many lessons in life and design, and we still remain friends all these years later.

Steve Louie, Interior Designer

Throughout the forty years that I have known Ruth, she has been many things to me. Starting in 1972, when I first met her as a student from Pratt, she entered my life and took on many roles. To this day, our relationship continues to evolve and grow.

To date, Ruth has been:

My Counselor: When I had joined the student chapter of the ASID, Ruth, along with other professionals, came to the Pratt Institute, where I was a student. She introduced herself as one of the Industry Counselors for ASID. She was the very first professional that I ever met.

My Conspirator: Every lecture or symposium that Ruth would encourage us to attend, we would conspire to question, challenge, and provoke all speakers. It was part of her DNA to cultivate inquisitive minds.

My Collaborator: After gaining several years of working experience, I was invited by Ruth to be her collaborator in designing residences for her clients. I quickly learned how different they were from corporate clients. With residential clients, we seemed to be part marriage counselors and part therapists.

My Confidant: During the period when I endured personal problems with my own marriage, Ruth extended her wisdom in guiding me through.

My Client: When Ruth acquired a new residence, I was flattered when she asked that I be her designer. Even in this different relationship, she proved to be the dream client that made the design process a joy.

My Companion: I can think of no greater honor, than to be able to shout to the world, that Ruth has been part of my life. There is no greater friend or companion.

John A. Lijewski, Interior Designer
President, Workplace Design Consultancy
Ruth Lynford has had a profound impact on my professional life since she picked me out of a crowd of young students to join her efforts as Student Education Chair of ASID. During my junior year as a young student at Parsons School of Design, we had a team project which involved three major design challenges facing New York City: redesign of the 14th Street Subway

> "Ruth led me to understand the importance of being involved with my fellow designers in a professional organization, where the goals of improving the profession by providing continuing education and a forum for discussion of critical issues, occur."

Station, redesign of Union Square Park, and redesign of the façade of S. Klein Department Store. All three of these projects were undertaken with the cooperation of the MTA, the Mayor's Office, and the local Community Board. The projects were year long with periodic reviews of all the stakeholders.

At the conclusion of the project, another team member and I were asked to present the team's recommendation to the Stakeholder Group. As Chair of ASID's Student Education Committee (SEC), Ruth was one of the invited guests. The presentation took place in the Parsons Auditorium with three hundred people in attendance. It was at the conclusion of this presentation that Ruth Lynford came up to me, congratulated me, and took me by the arm and said, "You need to attend a meeting of fellow students." The meeting was to be held the following evening at her office where she wanted me to meet several other students from New York design schools. At the time, there was no option. Her enthusiasm for my presentation and for the students that she had gathered together tweaked my interest. So, the following evening after classes, I attended my first of many meetings with Ruth and the group of students. The group was the Student Education Committee (SEC) of the American Society of Interior Designers, (ASID). From that first meeting, I was engaged in a long career of involvement with my fellow students soon to become the future leaders of our profession. We, collectively, with Ruth's leadership did great things to promote the value of design education and the value to students of belonging to ASID. With Ruth's guidance and encouragement, I went on to become President of the SEC, and later joined the International Interior Design Association, (IIDA), which was more aligned with my professional interests in commercial design. Eventually, I became president of the New York Chapter and on to be the International President of IIDA. To this day, I continue my commitment to the profession and serve as Chair to the Counsel for Interior Design Education (CIDA), the accrediting body for interior design programs in colleges and universities throughout the United States and Canada.

Ruth led me to understand the importance of being involved with my fellow designers in a professional organization, where the goals of improving the profession by providing continuing education and a forum for discussion of critical issues, occur. This is of utmost importance to me. Now, over forty years later, I continue to value the work done by professional design organizations. Had it not been for Ruth and her mentorship of me, I would not have had the opportunities and experiences that allowed me to truly love the profession I have chosen. As a professional, I continue to enjoy the satisfaction of knowing I helped create environments that made life better for those who lived and worked in them.

Texture and Shape | 133

Bryan English, Interior Designer

I met Ruth while I was studying design at Pratt Institute. She became my mentor and quickly a life-long friend. We have served on many committees together and collaborated on numerous design projects.

One experience always makes me laugh when I think of it. In 1974, we were attending the National ASID Convention in Denver, Colorado, and Ruth was made a Fellow of the ASID at a gala affair at the Denver Hilton. After the event, a group of us went to a party being held on the roof of the hotel. I was talking with some people when Ruth turned to me and asked if I would hold her watch. The next thing I hear is the splash of Ruth jumping into the pool in her evening gown!

To me, this event says everything about this extraordinary woman. One minute she is being acknowledged for her achievements and service to others and the next minute, the little girl comes out and she is swimming in an evening gown. A truly amazing woman! I am very lucky to call her a friend.

> "I was talking with some people when Ruth turned to me and asked if I would hold her watch. The next thing I hear is the splash of Ruth jumping into the pool in her evening gown!"

Andrea Roberts, LCSW, Client

As I reflect on design journeys since 1965, in three consecutive homes representing stages of my life, from new mother to seasoned grandmother, I see Ruth. Always an encouraging presence, she has been so much more than the consummate professional; she has become a true friend. In the face of confusion, when I have had to make sometimes difficult, exciting choices, she has managed to simplify the process by saying, "Always remember, Andrea, to ask yourself this, Does it please me?" These words have served me well!

In the course of living, there are those rooms that one can pass through, even pause to admire and eventually forget. Ruth Lynford's designs, like the designer, are unforgettable, a celebration of, and respect for, each client's individuality, replete with Ruth's own, inimitable, fine stamp of distinction. They resonate truth and integrity, pragmatism and accessibility, vibrancy and warmth, agelessness, and timelessness. Lacking all pretense, they never cease to charm. Each, like Ruth, is a classic beauty, and a gift to all of us.

Beverly Russell, Author, Journalist

United States President Calvin Coolidge spoke about the universal power of persistence. Ruth Lynford not only demonstrates persistence, but also determination and total confidence in her goal to fully recognize interior design as a profession alongside architecture.

Ruth and I marched forward together with this aim against very strong opposition in the 1980s and 90s. We gathered strength and support and in the process created some truly memorable events to raise funds for the cause. Their scale snowballed as we went along. How we did it, looking back, I just don't know. Ruth had a magic that made things happen. For one event, we persuaded Poltrona Frau, the estimable Italian furniture company whose New York office was run at the time by enthusiastic CEO James Goodwin, to give away loads of their luscious leather samples to about forty top interior and fashion designers. Each one was asked to create an original object for auction at a fundraiser for IDLNY. This made it very competitive. What an evening it was. I remember Jack Lenor Larsen's beautiful leather lampshades amongst the stunning pieces. I still have my prize—a fabulous box made of hundreds of chips of leather by fashion designer Nicole Miller. After that came an even more ambitious event, "Destinations" with collaboration from Steelcase. We invited seventeen top interior designers to use Steelcase furniture to create a round-the-world journey of different destinations. Somehow we talked the fashion mavens June Weir and Todd Oldham into contributing a fashion capsule.

These were just two of the many glorious collaborations spearheaded all the way by Ruth Lynford with her remarkable energy and drive. I was honored to hold her hand.

James Vaughan, Interior Designer, Educator

I consider Ruth an enduring inspiration, a mentor, and a dear friend. She is one of those people, whom one rarely meets, who leaves a lasting impression of exquisite style, charm, intelligence, and dynamic energy. She has accomplished so much in her lifetime by sheer vision, intelligence, and determination. We always say, "Once Ruth gets hold of something, she is like a pit bull, not letting go until it is completed."

"Some people inspire others by what they do; others, by the words they speak or write; and still others, by authentically being themselves. Ruth Lynford does all three."

I first met Ruth when I was just starting my own interior design business, incorporated under the name Related Designs. I was probably no more than twenty-eight years old. I joined the American Society of Interior Designers (ASID) and got involved with the Education Committee. Ruth was the chair of that committee and turned it into a dynamic forum on all "cutting edge" issues of design and design education. She would organize panel discussions that were riveting. Olga Gueft, editor of *Interiors* magazine, would publish excerpts from those meetings with pictures of Ruth and her distinguished guests. Ruth, all five feet of her, would appear with her usual large, bouffant, black hair, teased to perfection. She would be dressed in stunning suits or dressed by name couture designers with sparkling jewels on her fingers. The students who attended these meetings were caught off-guard by this tiny tornado with her keen insights and intellect. Some of these meetings would take place at Ruth's upstate home. Students were welcomed to her house, given a delicious lunch and plenty to feed on intellectually. Those were heady times that I shall never forget.

As a result of serving on this committee with Ruth, I met educators from the many design schools located in and around New York City. It was they, along with Ruth, who encouraged me to try my hand at teaching. My first class was a business course at Pratt Institute. I loved it.

Even though I was only in my thirties, I felt there was so much I wanted to share with the students. Subsequently, I taught at New York University and finally at the Fashion Institute of Technology. During my thirty years in the academic world, Ruth was always involved in furthering the professional level of design education. Many times she came as a critic at my students' presentations. During my time as Chairperson of the Interior Design Department at FIT, Ruth spearheaded New York Eleven, an exhibit of student work from all the design schools in New York. This tied in to her work with the state government in Albany. Her idea was to show the politicians the high level of knowledge and understanding that design students were getting, including the health, safety, and welfare of the public. The student work was always spectacular and the exhibit was open to the public. Students saw what the other schools were doing and sometimes switched to what they thought was a better school. The state lobbyists and politicians were able to see interior design was not just slipcovers and curtains, and the public had an introduction to the fantastic ideas and remarkable presentation skills of future, professional interior designers. It was a win, win, win, and Ruth was the one who made it happen.

I was fortunate enough also to work with Ruth on the design of her Fifth Avenue apartment across from Central Park. It all started innocently enough. Ruth, Su Yen Chue, and I succeeded in transforming the interior into a glamorous New York apartment. One big asset was a spectacular view of the park. We created a beautiful backdrop for Ruth's elegant art collection. However, there was one painting that I felt just did not work. I told Ruth that the space would be better off without the intense green that dominated the painting. It turned out that the painting was of sentimental value to her. Some months later, when I arrived for a party, I noticed the painting had found its way out into the elevator foyer, where Ruth had persuaded the other tenant on the floor to let her oversee the selection and placement of artwork.

It was at this same apartment that we attended one of Ruth's many birthday parties. We knew most of her family and friends who were there to honor her. However, a few hours into the evening, a strong, tall, young woman with an interesting accent came sweeping into the gathering. No one seemed to know who she was. We persuaded one of Ruth's grandchildren to go and find out who this mystery woman could be. Well, it turned out to be Ruth's personal trainer. At that time, Ruth was well into her eighties. Who knew she had an exercise trainer!

What I admire about Ruth is that she is a no-nonsense, let's-get-it-done type of person. She does not get involved with petty disagreements. She is a clear thinker and a visionary. She does not take things personally. She is generous to a fault. I have been the recipient of many lovely lunches and dinners. My wife and I shall never forget being invited to dinner and dancing at the Metropolitan Club near Ruth's apartment. It was an exquisite setting. Everyone was dressed to the tees and a small orchestra played in the background. But what was most memorable of all was what was seen through the large windows that fronted on Central Park. It had just begun to lightly snow with small flecks of white softly falling through the black of night. Through the snowflakes, we could glimpse the bright orange fabric hung from the many, repetitive, large, gate-like structures winding their way all through the park, part of the monumental work of the famous conceptual artist Christo. It was magical. I am blessed to have Ruth as a friend.

Kerwin Kettler, Educator

While I had heard rumors, the official note on her honorary Doctorate of Fine Arts Degree from the New York School of Interior Design struck me deeply. Of all the honors that she has collected, I personally believe that this one strikes to her core as one of the sharpest intellectuals in the design world today; and I am in a position to know, and appreciate this. At the root, it is her mind, not her energy and "get done" drive, which sets her aside from the crowd. It is so exciting, so deserved!

Dr. Debbie Joffe Ellis, Psychologist

Some people inspire others by what they do: others, by the words they speak or write; and still others, by authentically being themselves. Ruth Lynford does all three. I have only known Ruth for a couple of years, and yet it feels to me as if I have known her for much longer— our friendship having quickly become one of substance, caring, and enjoyments shared. She now welcomes me as practically one of her family, which brings me great joy.

I first saw her in 2010, when I attended one of the ICIS Salon meetings she hosts in her home. Though I knew nothing about her at that time, I was immediately impressed by her graciousness, poise, and vibrant energy. We first spoke at length when she and the President of ICIS invited me soon after to present at one of the Salon evenings. Again, I was impressed. Her genuine interest in, and enthusiasm for what I could share at such an evening was most encouraging and warming.

> "Visionary, generous, committed, vivacious, enthusiastic, knowledgeable, determined, sharp, gracious, interested, engaged, and resourceful: these are just a few of the adjectives which begin to describe Ruth."

When the occasion came, the room was full—all seats were occupied and additional attendees were standing in all available spaces. What a surprise to see Ruth sit in front of me for the whole ninety minutes on a tiny footstool, her back perfectly straight, and I mean perfectly, shoulders back in healthy posture. Looking up at me, she focused intently on every word I was saying. As a practitioner of yoga, I noticed such things. Not once did I see her shuffle or shift her position; comfort, centeredness, and a natural ease and elegance was, and is, her style.

Ruth is an inspiration through what she does, says, and is.

Doing: Ruth is one of the most active people I know. She tirelessly pushes to enable improvements as evident in her ongoing work on seeking recognition and rightful status for her field of interior design. She is also on the ICIS committee, helping to plan and arrange its events and activities, and additionally generously provides her living room space for presentations. She continues to encourage and support the ideas and ideals of people she believes in. For example, at a recent ICIS meeting, a young architect spoke about his desire to create more caring hospital environments, Ruth made it clear, with great enthusiasm about the things she will do to help him and his colleagues achieve the noble goals and mission. She also takes ongoing interest in her family members and close friends and gleefully expresses delight when others share good news, and shows great empathy when hearing about news of a less positive nature. Simultaneously, she makes time for an interesting, stimulating social life, attending operas and the like. Through her disciplined exercise workouts, she also keeps herself in good health and vitality.

Saying: When Ruth speaks, she engages the listener. She has substantial knowledge about many things and shares what she knows, has recently discovered, or that which she observes in the present, with absorbing clarity of expression. She listens very intently and well—a quality which only the best of communicators demonstrate. Her questions are thoughtful and at times thought-provoking, and show how well she has heard and understood what the person speaking to her has shared. And when she speaks of happy events or experiences—either her own or those of another—the genuine joy in her voice is uplifting in itself.

Being: A teacher of science once told me that when one strikes a tuning fork so that it makes the sound of C, and another tuning fork is put in its vicinity without even striking it, it will take on the vibrations, sound, and resonance of the first tuning fork, simply by being in its proximity. Ruth Lynford resonates thoughtfulness, elegance, impeccable style, good taste, beauty, caring, intelligence, interest, enthusiasm, and *joie de vivre*. In her company, I, and others whom I have observed, feel inspired. We may

Texture and Shape | 139

not, unfortunately, take on all her qualities automatically, a-la-tuning fork, but we feel refreshed, enlivened, and uplifted having been in the presence of this outstandingly fine woman.

Sarajane Brittis, Ph.D., President, ICIS

Visionary, generous, committed, vivacious, enthusiastic, knowledgeable, determined, sharp, gracious, interested, engaged, and resourceful: these are just a few of the adjectives which begin to describe Ruth Lynford—a woman extraordinarily dedicated to the individuals and professionals she befriends and organizations she serves.

She has been in the forefront in identifying key trends, not only in architecture and design fields, but also with regard to the social, political, and humanitarian issues facing the world. She has played a leadership role in bringing people together to address the issues.

As a Corporate and Board member of ICIS for nearly forty years, Ruth has been, from the start, an integral member of the ICIS team, adeptly using her amazing social and networking skills to bring together leaders in various fields to address issues of public concern. For example, early in her association with ICIS during the 1970s, she used her architectural and interior design skills to help redesign a sixty-thousand-square-foot building, which was being developed by ICIS group members as a facility with comprehensive youth services to help support young people living in New York. Taking a "whole person" approach, "The Door," as the Center became named, provided integrated programs and services in the areas of health, mental health, education, careers, law, social services, performing and graphic arts, and physical fitness. While her initial association with ICIS and The Door began on a tour of the facility, she became immediately interested in the goals and activities at the Center. Seeing that she could help contribute architectural

"She truly enjoys life, and in the process, she positively impacts so many lives by her leadership, integrity, and example."

and design expertise, she used her connections with the leaders of architecture and design schools in New York City to get them civically involved in the design of the new structure, while also getting furniture contributed to the new Center. As a result of her efforts and expertise, combined with the programmatic vision of the other ICIS team members, The Door became a national and international model of youth development and comprehensive youth services.

Ruth has also taken a leadership role in ICIS Salons, a key outreach activity of ICIS, which has the purpose of bringing people together from diverse fields and perspectives. Over the past ten years, she has hosted over fifty Salons in her home on wide-ranging topics including science and consciousness, the possibilities and limits of forgiveness, creativity as manifested through poetry, music, collage, and photography, the Rwandan genocide, poverty, hope, anger, love, diversity, and the work of antebellum African-American artists. Most recently, she spearheaded a three-part series on climate change bringing together architects and professionals from the United Nations with whom she had worked, to address the issues of climate change, especially as it relates to the New York experience. The breadth of these Salon topics indicates that Ruth has a highly developed social/global consciousness and encourages the exploration of different themes.

Ruth is a doer and totally action-oriented. Throughout her life, she has used her expertise and knowledge to advance causes which are of professional and personal concern to her. However, what makes her unique is her ability to transcend role stereotypes. She approaches all her activities with vitality, kindness, grace, warmth, and enthusiasm. She truly enjoys life, and in the process, she positively impacts so many lives by her leadership, integrity, and example.

Representative List of Projects

Commercial Spaces

Amend & Amend, Attorneys
Pearl River, New York

Apawamis Golf & Country Club
Rye, New York

Bader's Hotel
Spring Valley, New York

Beach Point
Palm Beach, Florida

Dr. Jeffrey Benjamin
Stamford, Connecticut

Blair & Co., Investment Brokers
New York, New York

Blantyre Castle Hotel
Lenox, Massachusetts

L. Paul Brief, MD, PC.
Spring Valley, New York

Century National Bank & Trust Co.
New York, New York

Chris-Ann Motel
Jersey City, New Jersey

Consolidated Stamp Co.,
Consolidated Foods Division
Spring Valley, New York

Milton Cooper, DDS
Hackensack, New Jersey

Cosco, Consolidated Foods Divison
Yonkers, New York

J.P. Dexter
Spring Valley, New York

Bertram P. Droga, MD, PC.
New City, New York

Florentina Restaurant
Nyack, New York

Franklin Society Federal Savings & Loan
Pearl River, New York

John Goebel, DVM
New City, New York

I. Grenadier, DDS
Mount Vernon, New York

Harder Hall Hotel
Sebring, Florida

Hilton Hotel
Long Boat Key, Florida

Jade Lantern Restaurant
Blauvelt, New York

New City Office Plaza
New City, New York

Oradell Savings & Loan
Oradell, New Jersey

Patricia Murphy Restaurant
Westchester, New York

Pearl River Savings & Loan
Pearl River, New York

Plaza Hotel, Guestrooms &
Private Suites
New York, New York

Arthur Schmidt Jr., President and
Chairman of the Board
Empire National Bank

C.J. Walters, MD
Westwood, New Jersey

Residential Spaces

Dr. and Mrs. Richard Adler
Buffalo, New York

Mr. and Mrs. M. Ansell
Haworth, New Jersey

Mr. and Mrs. Percy Auerbach
*Spring Valley, New York &
Fort Lauderdale, Florida*

Mr. and Mrs. Ayala
Hewlett, New York

Beach Point
Palm Beach, Florida

Mr. and Mrs. Donald Benjamin
Montvale, New Jersey

Dr. and Mrs. Jeffrey Benjamin
North Stamford, Connecticut

Mr. and Mrs. Kenneth Bergenfeld
New City, New York

Mr. and Mrs. Alan Blankstein
Suffern, New York

Mr. and Mrs. Jerome Bonat
Fort Lee, New Jersey

Mr. and Mrs. John Borressen
Wood Ridge, New Jersey

Mr. and Mrs. Charles Brennauer
New York, New York

Mr. and Mrs. William F. Bristow
West Nyack, New York

Mr. and Mrs. Martin Brown
Ridge Wood, New Jersey

Dr. and Mrs. Paul Brief
West Nyack, New York

Dr. and Mrs. Milton Cooper
*Tenafly, New Jersey &
Wycoff, New Jersey*

Mr. and Mrs. William Crowley
Ramsey, New Jersey

Mr. Seymour Deutsch
New York, New York

Mr. and Mrs. Harold Driscoll
Suffern, New York

Dr. and Mrs. Bertram P. Droga
New City, New York

Mrs. Elaine Faulkner
Valley Cottage, New York

Dr. and Mrs. John Goebel
New City, New York

Mr. and Mrs. Roy Gold
*New City, New York &
Pottsville, Pennsylvania*

Mr. and Mrs. Christopher Hall
Chappaqua, New York

Projects | 143

Mr. and Mrs. Karl Hammer
Tenafly, New Jersey &
Lakewood, New Jersey

Mr. and Mrs. Martin Infante
Ridgewood, New Jersey

Mr. and Mrs. Joseph Kurland
Nyack, New York

Mr. and Mrs. Stephen Kurland
Spring Valley, New York

Mr. and Mrs. Dale Leam
Irvington, New York

Mr. Martin Mazur
New York, New York

Dr. and Mrs. George Menken
New City, New York

Mr. and Mrs. Randall Motland
Mount Kisko, New York &
Greenwich, Connecticut

Mr. and Mrs. Joseph Muscarelle
Hackensack, New Jersey

Mr. and Mrs. Joseph Muscarelle, Jr.
Saddle River, New Jersey

Dr. and Mrs. J. Neiman
New City, New York

Mr. and Mrs. Hugh Newman
Wood Ridge, New Jersey &
Boca Raton, Florida

Dr. and Mrs. O'Brien
Demarest, New Jersey

Mr. and Mrs. Ornsten
Wilmington, Delaware

Mary Emily Price
New York, New York

Ms. Gloria Prisament
Hastings-on-Hudson, New York

Mr. and Mrs. Norman Prisament
Dobbs Ferry, New York

Andrea Roberts
Piermont, New Jersey

Mr. and Mrs. Walter Rutherford
Chappaqua, New York

Mr. and Mrs. Arthur Schmidt Jr.
Chester, New York; Nanuet, New York;
& Southbury, Connecticut

Mr. and Mrs. Sherwin Slater
New City, New York

Mr. and Mrs. Roland Thomas
Stony Point, New York

Joan Throckmorton and Sheldon Satin
Pound Ridge, New York

Mr. and Mrs. Claude Vanderbroek
Haworth, New Jersey

Dr. and Mrs. C. J. Walters
Pearl River, New York

Mr. and Mrs. George Winnie
Oradell, New Jersey

Dr. and Mrs. D. Zeller
Washington, D.C.

Awards and Recognition

Bachelor of Architecture Degree from Washington University, St. Louis, Missouri

Honorary Doctorate Degree from the New York School of Interior Design

Distinguished Alumni Award from Washington University, Founder's Day

Distinguished Alumni Award from Washington University School of Architecture

Leadership Award of Excellence, International Interior Design Association (IIDA), New York Chapter

Licensed as an Interior Designer in New York State

President of Lynford Ltd., a firm specializing in institutional, commercial, and residential interior design.

Fellow of American Society of Interior Designers

Associate Member of American Institute of Architects

Founding President of Interior Designers for Legislation in New York (IDLNY)

Responsible for the creation of Interior Design as the thirty-third profession in New York State

Founder of New York Eleven Plus

Member of the Board of Directors of the Association for the Study of Man/ Environmental Relations

Member of the American Institute of Architects (AIA)

Lecturer on the psychological and physical effects of the built environment

Lectured to students of all New York schools on the importance of licensing in New York State.

Served as a critic of school thesis projects at Fashion Institute of Technology and the New York School of Interior Design.

Leader in the effort to promote Sustainable Architecture and Interior Design

Designated "Most Excellent" by Officeinsight in recognition of her ardent and continuous efforts to create public and legislative awareness of the contributions of interior designers to the health, safety, and welfare of the public

Inducted Member of the Interior Design Hall of Fame

Serves on the National Advisory Council of Washington University School of Architecture

Serves on the Washington University New York Regional Cabinet

Serves on the Washington University Eliot Society

Serves on the Board of Advisors of Fashion Institute of Technology

Serves on the Board of Advisors of Pratt Institute

Serves on the Board of Advisors of New York Institute of Technology

Serves on the Board of Directors International Center for Integrative Studies (ICIS), a non-governmental organization of the United Nations

Serves on the Board of International Council of Caring Communities (ICCA), a non-governmental organization of the United Nations

Served on the Advisory Council of Cornell University

Served as National Chairperson of Education for American Society of Interior Designers (ASID)

Served on the Consortium of Environmental Behavior with the Federal Government

Designed Furnishings for Pierre Cardin's "Environments for the Home"

Published in *Interiors, Interior Design, House & Garden,* and *New York Interior Design Masters of Modernism*

Cited for contributions to the Interior Design profession in *Women of Design,* by Beverly Russell

Selected as a "Design Icon" by *Interior Design* magazine

Recognized by the New York State Assembly for a Lifetime of Good Service to the State of New York as a visionary as well as a strong political advocate in the field of interior design

Acknowledgements

This book and its design came about from the sweet inspiration of so many people. Knowledge from Gyo Obata pointed the way. During the building process, the Birkman and McKendy families helped shape the foundation: Beverly, Tom, Annie, and Katherine McKendy and Ellen, David, Jonathan, and Joseph Birkman. Close friends, Susan Blair Bennett and Robert Herrmann provided five-star support and shelter during construction. Heartfelt thanks to each of you.

Dear friends Mary Strauss and Jenny Ross Manganaro nudged me forward with readings about Sister Parrish, Dorothy Draper, and Madeleine Castaing, and soon I had a frame. As I sprang into action, so many others with whom I stir up joy, helped me to complete the structure: Dr. James Ziegler and family, Jan Greenberg, Mary and John Krogness, Lynn and Bob Rubright, the Bullocks, the Von Weises, the Kidos, the Fluris, Joanie Glassman, Helane Rosenberg, Dianne Koehnecke, Araceli Kopiloff Zimmer, George Shea, Phyllis Wilkenson, Sarah Whitney, Debbie Stiles, Gay Ackerman, Susan Grigsby, Stellie Siteman, Silvia Navia, Sydne Brown, and Suze Katzman. To you, I say, "Thank you."

Special thanks also to Dr. Brenda Fyfe, my Dean at Webster University, and to all my colleagues and students. I extend ongoing gratitude to Dr. Ted Green, my friend, who helped me maintain momentum. To Terry Lynford, who transcribed the tapes and stood by my side during the process, I give a standing ovation.

In addition, I am deeply appreciative of the genius and support of Kiku Obata and Kiku Obata and Company, especially Amy Knopf, for their creative design and total engagement throughout the process. I also applaud Images Publishing Group, for bringing our efforts to life. Thank you, as well, to Shelley Bennett for her keen and caring eyes on the copy and Ruth Novoa and Dorina Christache for their New York welcome and assistance.

And to Ruth Lynford, my exemplar, who not only taught me the importance of truth and beauty, but also the power of the quick-step, I shout, "Encore." Her size five footwork ever inspires and lights the way.

Photography Credits

Thank you to the following photographers whose photos appear in this book:

Schweig, St. Louis – p. 16
Pemberton Studios – p. 18
Unknown – p. 20
Unknown – p. 22, top
Murillo – p. 22, bottom
Unknown – p. 25
Geo W. Redden Photographic Co. – p. 26
Block Ross – p. 29
Dieckman (St. Louis) – p. 31, top
Unknown – p. 31, bottom
Wilsor Todd – p. 32
Behrens-Unterberger Photographers – p. 33
Unknown – pp. 36, 41
HaviLand – p. 43
Aura Studios, N.Y. – p. 45
Master Portraits – p. 46
Unknown – p. 49
The Journal-News – p. 51
Master Portraits – p. 52
Charlotte-Lee Studio – p. 54
Paula Stone – p. 60
Steven Louie – pp. 62–63
Greg Hall – pp. 65, 66, 69, 70, 73
Master Portraits – p. 74
LSI Industries / Lightron Company – pp. 78, 81–86
Archive Pierre Cardin – p. 80
Unknown – pp. 90, 104
Kevin Tavarez – p. 102
Sarajane Brittis – p. 108
Christopher Sturman – pp. 116, 123, 130
Unknown – p. 119, top
Joel Greenberg – p. 119, bottom

A Note on Typography

This book was set in Univers and Helvetica Neue. Univers was designed by Adam Frutiger in 1957 and first released by the Deberny & Peignot foundry in Paris, the design is a neo-grotesque, similar to its contemporary, Helvetica. With the release of Univers, Frutiger began using numbers rather than names to designate variations of weight, width, and slope. Frutiger used this system on a variety of other designs including Serifa and Frutiger.

Helvetica Neue is a twist on the original Helvetica font, which was designed by Max Miedinger in 1957. The original Helvetica was created as a sans-serif face to compete with Akzidenz-Grotesk in the Swiss market. Helvetica Neue was released by AG Linotype in 1983. This new version improved the appearance, legibility, and usefulness of the original version.

Much of the information provided in this book is based on the personal memories and recollections of Ruth Lynford. We have made every effort to portray events, individuals, companies, and products accurately. In addition, we have made extensive efforts to trace the original source of copyrighted material contained in the book. While Ruth Lynford and Autobiographical Publishing Company Pty Ltd. believe that all rights have been obtained to reproduce, exhibit, display, and distribute the original works of authorship made by third parties that are included in the book, we welcome hearing from any copyright holders. Ruth Lynford, the publisher, and the author accept no responsibility for errors, omissions, or misrepresentations, and they specifically disclaim all warranties, express or implied, related to the material in the book, including without limitation, accuracy, merchantability, or fitness for a particular purpose.